YOU ARE
HISTORY

YOU ARE HISTORY

The Soul, The Higher Self, and our Share of Divinity

by

GORDON PHINN

The Eternal Life Trilogy, Part 3

www.whitecrowbooks.com

CONTENTS

INTRODUCTION

Y*ou Are History* is the third part of my Eternal Life Trilogy, an out-of-body adventure I've been detailing since 1999. With part one, *Eternal Life And How To Enjoy It,* I and my guide Henry moved about some of the spirit planes, encountering the various inhabitants, landscapes and societies they found themselves in. My conscious intention had been, after many decades of sporadic astral trips, many only half recalled in the morning, to take advantage of my surprising new levels of lucidity and put together a guide for the modern seeker, as many of the older Spiritualist communications then seemed fusty and old fashioned, to say the least. I wound up with something of a guided tour of the Afterlife realms, with many characters and situations previously uncovered by either mediumistic channeling or automatic writing, but updated to our post-feminist, post-modern, post irony and privacy and indeed, post-anything world. This was the dead-and-loving-it version of modernity, without the terrors of damnation and hell, the hang-ups about sex and the illusions of national pride and glories of pointless sacrifice fostered by scheming politicians and aristocrats. As readers saw, people there are not much different from people here: lovers reunite in sensual pleasure, families congregate as they pass over and continue their group consciousness, souls explore and learn, freed from the inhibitions and erroneous assumptions their counterparts brought over to the astral a century ago.

The following excerpts will convey some of the flavor:

"I hope such bald faced discussion of astral plane sexuality has not offended anyone, but I am determined to break the hold religionists have had on channeled communications for the last century or so. The poor souls meant well, but they managed to convey totally erroneous notions of asexual angels gliding about praising the lord and doing good works, when in fact, most souls are very sensual here, as joy is constantly in the air and there are no strictures or punishments for acting out your desires.

No disease, no pregnancy, no shame."

"Alex and Hershel are golfing partners from way back. Heck they've been dead almost as long as me. They're 71 and 73 respectively. Alex from a heart attack after his Vietnam vet son committed suicide and Hershel from good old-fashioned cancer. Only Hershel's wife is here, and only just: She hung in till she was 89. Hershel thought she was nuts ; all those years in that nursing home when she could have been here having fun. He tried to convince her – God knows how many times – while she was asleep. But she did love her grandchildren and her great-grandchildren. Hershel says it's the matriarch complex – convinced the ship of state can't run without you. Now she wants to enlarge the house to make more space for family when they come. Hershel tells her they can have their own houses; hell this place is bigger than Texas and New Mexico put together, but she's consulting with a renovator and interior designer now. She really is in Heaven, he laughs, but she still won't admit she shoulda come here sooner."

In that first exploration I did have some notions of Higher Self/ Monad that were explored towards the end of the narrative (and will be recapped later here). But my basic grasp on that being/consciousness was greatly developed in part two, *More Adventures In Eternity*, where Higher Self contributed on several occasions to the progress of that multidimensional series of narratives. HS, as I came to call it, became an animated persona in a large cast of characters, including prophets like Maitreya and Buddha, past lives, future selves and all manner of dead folk filing reports from their comfort zones.

This was something of a pleasant surprise to the questing author, as, like many aspirants on the path, I assumed a linear ascent to dizzying heights was in order. One sees the bold exploration of the astral that is the product of lucidity and one pointed focus as some necessary step to the unfolding of those higher and higher levels where the average dead person fears to tread. One fails to take into account that the multidimensional nature of the universe which consciousness creates, forgets and then explores, allows for unscheduled irruptions by the likes of angels and Higher Selves. Like babies who arrive when they feel like it rather than the convenience of parents, spirit beings do not operate as we might prefer. Synchronicity is but one of their little tricks.

Trying to reconcile the aspirant's dearly held notions of ordered progress and understandable unfoldment with the delirious, crazy quilt anarchy of Spirit and the beings who tempt us into immersing ourselves in it, can be a daunting task; one that I attempted in the introduction to, winding up with formulations like this:

"As pointed out by entities such as Seth (and others), Higher Self exists not in time but eternity and, amongst other attributes, experiences its various expressions (incarnations) as simultaneous, and not as the linear cause-and-effect implied by past life regression studies. However useful and instructive past life regressions are, the involution/evolution journey of that 'divine spark from the godhead' discussed by many systems seems quite inoperative from the point of view of Higher Self. To the reincarnating personality, the relationships, traumas and ecstasies of past lives can seem all too real and relevant to currently experienced situations and, as a therapeutic and educative tool, their value to the psyche is unimpeachable. But to Higher Self such reparations may be little more than timely first aid. Higher Self seems endlessly fascinated with combining and recombining various energies into packets of information which function as psychic templates for incarnate personalities to express their always evolving reactions to the challenges posed by physical plane existence.

"In a sentence, Higher Self sees things one way while incarnate personality sees things another way. Will there be a blending of perspectives? I sure hope so; 'physical Gordon' has been chiseling out his response for years. The progress report looks like this:

"As the incarnate personality continues to expand, its perceptions overflow their original dimension. What was once defined by space (a body), becomes defined by time (many bodies). What was once defined by physical plane reality (inevitable extinction) becomes redefined by astral plane reality (apparent immortality) and then further refined by Higher Self contact (eternity experienced in a huge variety of self-engineered limitations). And as a result the one track mind becomes the multidimensional being."

All aspirants develop, in the course of their self-directed educations, ideas on various topics covered by the literature they manage to access and the teachers who come their way. Those ideas tend to be covered in a kind of mystical remoteness which simultaneously preserves their innocence and encourages their lack of self-worth. And despite some individual variations I was not exempt from this. The deep, traditional roots of mystical and esoteric teachings stretch to Greece, Egypt and farther, and their tangled and complex delivery to our modern world, with all its skepticism and mocking repression, can easily reinforce the diminutive status of the student.

Take Professor Gregory J. Riley's *The River Of God* (2001), his history of Christian origins: - speaking of the rise of monotheism in Egypt, he says "If God was outside and infinite, then the cosmos must be inside God. Thus arose the idea of God as the container of the cosmos who was in turn contained by nothing. God was not in a place. But was the place in which all else was. This God came to be termed the Monad, the "One" (from the Greek word meaning "one alone"), who was the source of all else." And later,... "The Monad did not even have a spiritual body – that is, a localized and measurable body made of some spiritual substance, like the bodies of angels were thought to have."

Or Annie Besant's *The Ancient Wisdom* (1897): "This Self is the One, and hence is spoken of as the Monad, and we shall need to remember that this Monad is the outbreathed life of the Logos, containing within itself germinally all the divine powers and attributes." And later: "It is a state in which each is himself, with a clearness and vivid intensity which cannot be approached on the lower planes, and yet in which each feels himself to include all others, to be one with them, inseparate and inseparable." Then quoting Plotinus's description of a sphere, comparable to the 'Turiya' of the Hindus, in which "They likewise see all things...and they perceive themselves in others, for all things there are diaphanous, and nothing is dark and resisting but everything is apparent to every one internally and throughout. For light everywhere meets with light, since everything contains all things in itself. Each thing likewise is everything, and the splendour there is infinite."

In thus comparing Besant brings the seeker, such as I once was, to glimpse the deep lineage of esoteric teachings making their way to the more obscure repositories of the new age movement, where the ultra-curious can uncover them just beneath the best-selling fluff usually on offer. The same realization of deep roots is apprehended when the seeker discovers that the mainstream academic philosopher Leibnitz produced a work called *Monadology* some three centuries back, still studied today. Then you can take John Holman's advice, in *The*

Return Of The Perennial Philosophy (2008) that he was leaning on an earlier work *De Perenni Philosophia* (1540) by Agostino Steuco, or in De Purucker's *Fundamentals Of Esoteric Philosophy*, which claims he was influenced by the Flemish mystic Van Helmont, who in turn was inspired by Giordano Bruno, or maybe directly, from NeoPlatonism.

Jan Kinney, in his introduction to the anthology "The Inner West" (2004) underlines this multi-source contribution to the "Inner West's" compendium of esotericism: "It is an underground stream of experiential wisdom traditions (often called esoteric) that have flowed down through the centuries to the present day. And in calling it a stream I don't mean to imply that the esoteric traditions of Western culture compose a unified whole. Certain elements derive from the Hellenistic Neoplatonic philosophy of the early Christian era, others from medieval Jewish Kabbalah, others from Renaissance Hermeticism, and other from pre-Christian pagan religions. Even Islam, via its esoteric traditions preserved in Sufism, can be included as a component, through its interaction with Christian and Jewish schools in Moorish Spain between the eighth and fifteenth centuries and its presence in the Ottoman Empire from the fourteenth through the nineteenth."

And so the seeker goes, deeper and deeper into the mysterious past with study, or vertically, into her own experience, through the avenues of astral projection, lucid dream, yoga or mindfulness meditation, all of which can and do produce mystical experiences of a distinctly non-rational, non-linear quality, where occasional contact with the various realms and denizens of spirit can morph into daily (if you dare) interactions with ghosts, guides, angels, ascended masters and Monads. Which is where I eventually wound up, somewhere between finishing *More Adventures In Eternity* and this sequel before you now.

Monads/Higher Selves, all chips off the old block of the transcendent divinity that some limit to the term 'God' and others allow as 'the great creative principle of the universe' or 'all that is', is/are our most real self. It continually creates 'divine sparks' to descend into the physical for the experiences of the mineral, vegetable, animal and human lifestreams. Each of these divine sparks ensouls the form it inhabits and, in the case of humanity, becomes an individual soul. That soul is what we seek and hopefully find beneath the personas foisted on us by family, society and religion. But when we find it and see that it easily survives the transition to spirit that some call death, our journey is not complete, for Monad does not exist in the spirit realms of the happy dead in paradise. That, despite its joys and fulfilments, we must

5

transcend to reunite with our true selves, Higher Self/Monad, which nests us with unconditional love and then rejigs the various elements of your constitution for another raid on the dramatic comedy we call life. Your current incarnation is far from being wholly you. Nor are any of your past (or future) lives. We are all puzzle pieces in the big jigsaw consciousness markets as life.

And within that puzzle, the tower of babel where communication is trapped in language, harmonious relations inhibited by the suspicions of tribalism and the constant threat of the Other, explanations spring up, from shamans, religions and economic elites, as to the source of all the bother. These elaborate legends, often cobbled together with cunning and contemptuous lies, have sequestered human society down through the ages to the modern day, where various belief systems, whether of the traditional or post-modern technocratic stripe, insist that various Others have to be controlled and often decimated so that some version of heaven on earth may be given free reign. One of those legends, Gnosticism (an early rival of Christianity never fully eliminated) is the ancient belief that man's spirit is imprisoned in matter by a mischievous creator. Man is living underwater, it posits, ignorant of the light and air above, and if only he could swim to the surface this new dimension would be apparent. Knowledge of, and communication with, Monad/Higher Self can dispel such ignorance. As aspirants we can see just how we descended from the Monadic heights of spirit into the matter that we helped create eons ago, the physical plane that minerals, vegetables, animals and man was made for. We were not duped by any deities, minor or major; we ourselves set up the parameters, took a dive and then forgot. Blending yourself with the consciousness of Higher Self/Monad can be of immeasurable help in dissolving any similarly limiting belief system, whether religious or political.

Returning to 'Gordon's' journey of discovery; In the first two volumes of this trilogy, *Eternal Life and How To Enjoy It and More Adventures In Eternity* I, and my then guide Henry, explored the afterlife worlds, the process of reincarnation, the multidimensional nature of the soul and its activities, and the enigma of Higher Self/Monad. During *More Adventures In Eternity* I felt the presence of Higher Self regularly and allowed its consciousness to express itself in several 'mergings' so that the reader could get some glimpses of where 'I', as an explorer, might end up. I did feel, quite strongly, that the soul, my soul, your

6

soul, anyone's soul, being an emanation of Monad/Higher Self, a spark from the divine fire, was destined, at some point or other, to rejoin its source, merging with the many others in the group while retaining its individual status, that inimitable character cobbled together from the slings and arrows of outrageous fortune.

How exactly that paradox would smooth itself out into a singularity was a puzzle to me, the 'me' that appeared to be writing the books, although I sensed somehow that it would. Perhaps with a few intuitive leaps and a healthy dose of what the sceptics call magical thinking.

In the intervening years, it gradually occurred to 'me' that our repeated appearances on the planet in an extensive variety of guises, rounding out our educations at the behest of guides and karmic colleagues, constituted in a series of bit parts in many cultural and historical shifts, an undeniable presence in the winding corridors of time and space. We do not stand apart from history, as the blinders of our isolated egos and educations might suggest, we are, as the catalogue of our souls' unfolding implies, history. And once the floodgates of soul memory are discovered, unlocked and then infiltrated, we know that we are history, God bless our cotton socks.

This book is a record of one such unfolding. Whether you believe that we merely inhabit archetypes of behaviour, flourish for moments in fantasies of courage, glamour and riches, or actually inhabit the soul probes we uncover in our searches, matters little. I am not here to prove one viewpoint over another, but to illustrate the details of my personal discoveries. Such proofs can be reserved for courts of law and roistering debates in the media. As with many mystical experiences, most especially the out-of-body adventure, each of us must explore and discover for ourselves, which, I trust, will become your ambition after reading this text, and maybe the entire trilogy.

From an initial fascination with the afterlife, its many mansions, pleasures and pursuits, 'I' uncovered more and more of what seemed remarkably like attributes and talents developed in 'earlier' lives. Why, for example, did 'I' find retrieval and rescue work so easy to adapt to? Why did finding myself as not just one, but sometimes three or four orbs, dancing about giddily and then settling to various tasks in the planes, seem so, well, not unusual? Why did slipping into the formless energy planes seem like taking a quick dip in the pool, when other explorers shied away from it? Why did Maitreya and Buddha seem so approachable and gentlemanly? Why did this notion of 'taking to it like a duck to water' continually come up for me?

I finally guessed, like the proverbial horse to water, that I'd done it all before, maybe with different clothes, attitudes and passwords. Yes, I was gradually rediscovering buried talents. The mystery school *was me. As it is you*, if you care to dig deeply enough. Books, teachers, practices, all point out the way, but the destination is you, the expanded you, more like a cloud of textured light than an ambulatory being rigged out with reason and emotion.

Just today, someone asked me by email: if we, the soul, are projections from Higher Self, then from where does Higher Self originate? My current answer would be the Radiant Void, the Great Unmanifest, the Ground Of All Being, the Endless Sea of Divinity from which all answers and questions spring. But that could change. The Soul, the Higher Self, the Divine are all labels for experiences but when we merge completely with the experiences the labels are no longer necessary. But while we're thinking it over and wondering how much of our precious identities, cultures and achievements we have to give up, let us keep using them, as they are handy tools for contending with problems that appear ever so real.

I grappled with the mysteries and enigmas of *You Are History* for a number of years, putting it aside uncompleted until my confidence in its insights and significance resurfaced. In this period, a number of friends read the manuscript and declared themselves intrigued, but it was the enthusiasm and encouragement of Ian Lawton who finally boosted me back on track, making me wonder why I'd given up in the first place. By placing my ideas alongside several of the leading lights in the field, both past and present, as he did in his work *Supersoul,* he allowed me a wide perspective and necessary distance to see the text in its source and destination, and I can only be grateful for that.

Meanwhile, let us return for a mini-refresher course in transcendent consciousness to the Higher Self merges of *More Adventures In Eternity:* Number two feels like good fit:

Outside of time, outside of space, outside of relevance to cultures, religions, and political systems, I, and those like me, exist and have our beings. We are, we always have been, and always will be. Our eternal selves are circumscribed only by God, that immutable infinite consciousness out of which all creation comes. Planets are our playgrounds, galaxies, our outbacks. Options are innumerable, and we build what you might think of as our character by exercising as many of them as we feel we can handle. Endless experiments in multiple incarnation. Multiple simultaneous incarnation.

The thrill of power, the gloom of oppression. The excitement of youth, the serenity of age. The pride of riches, the shame of poverty. Adventures in the food chain. Ignorance and intelligence. Instinct, intellect, and intuition. All these and more are our game preserve. We send you out into them to collect experiences. You return to show us just how the varieties of fear and desire create their rigid systems of belief in which you inevitably settle or struggle, depending on the details and your perception of them.

Those of you who have followed the word thus far: we would like you to feel that you are us and can have the accumulated wisdom of our data banks at your fingertips, pretty much any time you wish. Exhausted with the illusion of power, we feel you are ready to access even more. Only now, at this juncture of the planet's evolution and yours, such knowledge breeds the understanding smile of humility rather than the reckless laugh of indulgence.

Earth matter now vibrates with a greater degree of freedom than ever before: the physical plane is about to take wing. We trust that you are inspired to fly with it, knowing that the harmonising of your so-called past sufferings enabled the slow severing of ancient bonds. You have paid for your enlightenment in full, friends! Please feel free to assume the new freedoms unfolding.

2

MOVIES

———————◆◆◆———————

I usually emerge from movies feeling that I have successfully escaped my life for a couple of hours and am ready to resume the role of 'Gordon' upon the physical plane in this country called Canada during this first decade of the new millennium. If the production is expertly crafted and lovingly brought to life by the technicians and actors, then my escape velocity is certainly tempered by an aesthetic rapture that coats my enthusiasm with an extra bliss, but the experience is primarily one of escape from personality into the bliss of non-being, where the desires and actions of humans are observed and absorbed by the manifest intelligence which loves to bathe in their reflections.

Of course, I used to say that I was an incurable film buff who loved the magic of the medium almost more than the myth of life itself, for that is how one is easily understood in regular society. Almost everyone understands how movies can become an addictive pleasure, not to mention a blessed relief from the pressures of a busy daily schedule. But the deeper, more spiritual dimension of movie watching is shared only with other movie fans. How the great directors, working with their creative teams, manifest a miniature universe on celluloid, is a miracle of no small stature, and film fans love to share their individual enthusiasms, rolling them into a collective ecstasy during the conversations where they carve their alternative realities.

Tonight, this October 28th, I suddenly realised, that this experience, this blissful escape from personality, is the model upon which I have calibrated my journeys into spirit, for each of those journeys was an escape from 'Gordon'. His striving personality, his suffering ego. While thus journeying, the experiencing "I", the indwelling soul now finally distinct from the crusading and isolated ego, knows that this earthbound character is little more than a bundle of attributes and tendencies fired by fear and desire, especially concocted for the timely resolution of various karmic projects by that transcendent intelligence I now know as Higher Self, or Monad.

The escape from personality powered by film is primarily an aesthetic one, the beauty and truth of the perceived elevating the experiencer to a Platonic realm where archetype and idea emerge as the major players in comedy-dramas of a very cosmic dimension. If the drama is executed with finesse, one watches enthralled as the designs of a minor deity unfold with precise timing and elemental grace. In the process one comes to understand how a world is sustained: through the constant creative effort we sometimes label 'love', but could easily answer the call of 'sustained problem-solving empathy' or 'determined and unrelenting custodianship'. Maybe we will stick with love.

The escape from personality powered by meditation or out-of-body projection is primarily an energetic one, although it certainly has aesthetic and spiritual elements to it. For although one may not immediately realise it, such explorations are powered by thought, which is the lowest, or most easily manifest of the divine vehicles. Thought is the propulsive force of all activity in the manifest worlds. Whilst the meditator/projector is experiencing on the astral levels, which of course, is the first and most common field of play, he feels and observes the force and effect of desire and is easily persuaded that the emotional body rules the territory. The astral planes, where fear, anger, joy and desire are experienced and fulfilled, are the proving grounds for such powerful illusions. With more experience the meditator/projector then comes to understand that it is actually thought which powers emotion, although the instantaneous effects are virtually indistinguishable to most experiencers on that level. Later, he comes to know how thought itself is stimulated, where intuition originates, and of the primary function of the causal body: they are all brought into being by the activity of Monad, that tiny planet of divine attributes which initiates and guides all our earthy and astral adventures. Its energetic connection to us, the people it provides with sustenance and recurring suspicions of purpose, are there to be discovered, utilised and expanded, and like all myths it benefits from intimate and prolonged exploration. This book is the record of a beginning to that exploration.

3

MONADS

———◆————

My Monad, or Higher Self to which 'Gordon' belongs, has made his/her presence and affections known in Part Two of the series, *More Adventures In Eternity,* and during the exposition of what can only be called the experiences of 'Gordon' 'Henry' and 'Higher Self, it became apparent to me that his repeated intrusions into the text were but an enticing foretaste of a more complete embrace in Part Three, where I felt that the individual (soul) consciousness would be simultaneously subsumed and expanded into the trans-dimensional omnipresence and likely near-omniscience of the Monad. I had several small tastes in meditation of this expansion and, even in retrospect, I cannot forget how daunted I was by the excitement.

To lose one's limited nature would be a great blessing but also a tremendous challenge in which the old Gordon, with all his attachments and issues, would virtually disappear. 'I' felt that I would welcome the change, but perhaps the shadow of the old Gordon would fight it all the way. That guy on the ground, with his shoes and coat and career– the physical elemental as I believe some Theosophists would term it– has a way of clinging to the known, and has developed a number of very subtle strategies to facilitate the continuation of his imprisonment. The rut-infested consciousness one might call it.

The ruts of personality based neuroses, the ones we despise but cannot seem to dispose of serve as our anchor in the harbour of reluctance,

reluctance to exchange self-defeating fears for the challenges of growth. We may feel timid, anxious, insecure, and reluctant to act in any way which disturbs the status quo of our lives and makes us face the reality that we are much more than our upbringing and society permits us to believe. We are light beings of almost infinite capacities, and more than likely multidimensional telepathic healers in disguise. Okay, but who's gonna manage my portfolio and get my kids through college? And what about yoga class and squash games? Can we maybe talk about this later, over drinks?

We are, in fact, fully qualified members of immensely intelligent group souls, Monads, which never in themselves descend into incarnation, but who can and do send many exploratory beams of energy down through the levels of spirit to that of the physical plane where they become, after acquiring (amongst others) causal, mental and astral bodies, a soul inhabiting a fetus inside a womb, then emerging as a baby to the world of blood, time and painful separation.

To reach back up, as the adult personalities which evolved from those babies, towards our source, and experience the consciousness of that source is the ultimate challenge and reward of physical plane existence. All other ambitions fade in its presence. As a project it must needs employ every talent acquired in previous growth projects. The loving embrace of the mother, the sacrifice of the father, the one pointed self-denial of the monk or the nun, the long hours and dedication to hard work of the trader and businessman, the careless play of the child, the convenient cunning of the politician, the patience of the teacher, the application of the student, all are employed in the calculated submission of pride and personality in the embrace of the wider consciousness of Higher Self/Monad.

All that you treasure about yourself and your attributes gets conveniently and temporarily trashed in your reach to rub out your signature and replace it with dozens of others. In the process you begin to understand *you are everyone* and *everyone is you* and that, to a large degree, having participated in most, if not all, of its stages you realise, *you are history.* You are the cast, the stars, the chorus, the cameos, and that there is little, if anything, in the human comedy-drama-mystery play that you do not know the essence of. How one does or does not sympathise with characters and the various conflict and resolution situations in movies is often a key to understanding one's own incarnational habitation of human archetypes. For example, if the clever escape from oppressive authority repeatedly intrigues then it is very likely one of 'your' especial issues, and exploring it may lead to the release of several energy blockages. But as you reach to merge with your Higher Self, you are effectively giving notice that you are about ready to retire from your career of parts, surrender their energetic attachments, and graduate to another level entirely. Of course it's considerably more intricate and cosmic, but we'll get to that later. The theatrical metaphor will do for now.

4

INITIATIONS

This reaching up/out to Monad/Higher Self, using soul energies to shape your path, is an inner journey with many stages, stages which can manifest in varying guises depending on the needs and expectations of the personality involved. These stages can also be seen as initiations, initiations in the traditional esoteric sense of gradual unveilings of greater and greater realities previously unimagined by the student.

Moving out from the recognised structures and ego based demands of the personality to the altogether more selfless embrace of the soul and its, shall we say, agenda, is the first of these initiations. Some students require a teacher to perform this unveiling, some a venerable and obscure tradition, some merely a congenial book that seems just to fall effortlessly into their hands. Once on the path of the soul, the student practices their daily discipline and adheres to the teachings as best they can, confident that their practice is appropriate and meaningful.

Some of the initiations experienced by the student are as much the result of astral plane activities percolating "down" into the physical level and activating various dormant psychic centres as they are of long term meditative practice, and the explosions of growth experienced, although shocking to the physical plane consciousness, are more or less natural outgrowths of astral plane "work".

For example, many of us have the repeated notion, if not actually lucid dream recall, that we are attending some sort of night-time class or training course. Although framed by the usual distortions of brain-based confusions, these are approximate renditions of actual long-term experience.

Many of us begin wandering the astral at night in a semi-conscious state, floating through various areas and densities, absorbing their energetic 'nourishment', which helps sustain us through the trials of the next day. We start by floating a few feet above our sleeping physical forms and then, if our innate curiosities outstrip our built-in anxieties, we move out, through the walls, roofs, or windows, into the night-time world beyond. Flying about the neighborhood and then countryside can amuse us for years. Some of us discover that intimate relationships can be sustained in this atmosphere, and those relationships can sometimes invade our domestic physical reality tunnels in ways that seem much more disruptive than congenial.

The permanent residents of the astral, the so-called dead, can often find ways of touching and communicating to us in these wanderings, and the quiet reassurance that so-and-so is "doing fine", which family members and friends often do not share, often arises from such interactions. These can lead to actual 'conscious' meetings in the astral communities in which our dear departed continue their lives, again resulting in vaguely reassuring memories of more youthful radiant faces and shared laughter in comfy parlors and remarkably lush gardens.

The next stage is often an exploration of those communities, most of which have classes for just such nocturnal visitors. Depending on the perceived needs and potential of the individual, these classes can vary greatly in depth and complexity, ranging from a basic outline of astral plane consciousness and what can be experienced within its parameters, to tightly focused self-development courses, where the student is trained to extend his/her consciousness to the more remote levels of spirit, most of which exist outside the vast majority of belief systems unconsciously carried around by the average astral explorer.

Those who participate in such unconscious night-time activities are often those who feel inexplicably drawn to the various self-development disciplines on Earth (meditation, yoga, etc.) and in the process find their progress periodically and mysteriously accelerated. Unusually transcendent states of consciousness, often accompanied by bursts of clairaudience or clairvoyance, erupt, amaze, and then quietly subside. They are warned by their teachers not to waste time wondering 'why', as such glamorous and elusive siddhis are a by-product of spiritual growth and not to be mistaken for its goal. Whether those teachers are merely reacting to the dictates of their chosen tradition or have enough active astral consciousness to know what is going on most likely varies from case to case, but the esoteric fact remains that, even for the partially awakened, effort expended on the astral results in various physical plane manifestations.

Pursued more consciously by the once-bewildered, now-emboldened Earth experiencer, this dual level of activity can result, if not in permanent astral consciousness then at the very least in an intuitive understanding of such a state. Effectively, this means an appreciation of the fact that the physical and astral are actually aspects/polarities of the same plane, the dark and light sides of the same coin, and that the common man's confusion and anxiety over the endless transitioning between the two is an illusion bred in ignorance and sustained by the mythmaking half-truths of religion.

Like all illusions, of course, it has its uses. Under it the evolving individual can develop the talents of courage, kindness, mercy and the like. But eventually, if that individual keeps progressing he/she will come to see that both planes are one and that the endless recycling of souls, regardless of the means of transition, is nothing to get excited about. Every second of every day throughout the entire history of this planet Earth, ensouled forms are arriving and departing, shuttling back and forth between the communities "there' and the communities "here". Their round trips are, in themselves, no more significant than a round trip ticket from New York to London. The traveller is gone for a while, has some experiences germane to their new location and level of participation, and then they return, with baggage of various types in tow. To see this is to be let in on a secret; to fully understand its significance is to be initiated.

Once across the threshold of that initiation, the seeker views life and their small part in it quite differently. For example, all sense of self-importance seems to quickly evaporate, as one comes to see that the drive for status and success is actually largely based on a subconscious fear of the meaninglessness imposed by the appearance of death, that final curtain which often fails to draw any applause.

As one surveys in meditation, or perhaps glimpses while walking or driving, the great new expanse of continuous experience unveiled with astral consciousness, one sees the infinity of growth available to the individual. One understands that all the tendencies and efforts of physical life are continued in astral life and there exists little or nothing which cannot be intelligently developed. One sees that all relationships can, and often are, continued on the so-called other side, and that the intermissions caused by 'death in time' are quickly forgotten when all are reassembled 'there'. One sees the suffering and knows that the agonies of wretched children cannot always be easily transmuted, and that pain has an evolutionary purpose equal to that of pleasure and joy. Most of all one feels sadness for the blindness brought on by ignorance and deep compassion for the sentient beings bound in fear.

How one translates that compassion into action is the first post-initiation project, and each attainee must improvise his/her own path. I know I'm improvising mine. If truth is a pathless land, as Jiddu Krishnamurti once so famously said, then compassion is perhaps a stormy ocean with many dangers and challenges. But individuals with even mere glimpses of astral consciousness understand that those dangers are but the shadow tigers of illusion, to be danced with rather than defeated. Dancing with those shadow tigers whilst others cower, or turn away in timidity or even displeasure and disgust more or less comes with the territory of compassionate action. The initiate's intuition will usually 'red flag' any individual ready for such intervention. Suddenly, as you're talking, you will know this person in front of you is there for a reason other than mere compliance with the norms of sociability. You wait, smiling and chatting, while the issue, or issues, makes itself known. Body language, a casual reference, a sick joke, an obsessive behaviour pattern, an illness still lingering, all are hints in the maze of social interaction, and the initiate must absorb the signals and sniff, like a dog in the breeze. Sometimes, you will see, as the issues unfold, the Roman Centurion, the Egyptian slave, the Cambodian monk, the Dutch trader, the English sailor press-ganged into service, the wife left bereft, the daughter pregnant or the son orphaned. Any, or several of these, might be the karmic source of the current energy blockage and life trauma/dilemma faced by the individual. Snippets of old dramas still active will play before your mind's eye, sometimes confusing with a plethora of hints.

One waits, one filters, one decides on a course of action. That action could range from a mere offer of friendship in a time of need, through healing in any of its many modalities, to careful instruction on such esoteric and maybe fantastical notions as 'past lives', 'karma' and 'pre-birth arrangements'. Sometimes the action devolves into occasional casual hints at stressful moments, often couched in joking banter. The student thus engaged must be ready to cope with public disapproval during scandals, family uproar during illness and dislocation, social outrage and political oppression when institutions and entrenched belief systems feel threatened; not to mention the odd sideways glance.

Depriving traditional belief systems of their fee-paying adherents can be a tricky business. Sinners and their minders like to strive for redemption; handing them your get-out-of-jail-free card can really upset the apple cart and hierarchies rarely take kindly to chasing the escaping fruit down anything that looks like a slippery slope. Yet assisting a striving soul to come to a personal understanding of the real state of things shorn of the myths of religion, politics, and sceptical materialism is usually worth it. The risk factor is not to be denied, but in most cases it can be assimilated into your game plan. You are rarely, if ever, handed a case beyond your current capabilities. You will be stretched, but not completely out of shape.

The initiation outlined above is a stage I had to pass through on my way to merging with Higher Self. I detail it as most of you will pass through something similar on this journey. It is not merely understanding that there is life after death, but that there is life after *that* life, too, and that it is merely another leg on an endless cyclical journey in and out of incarnation, thousands of years in linear time – a mere twinkling of an eye to Higher Self reality. It is also living from day to day as if that understanding were the core of your being, the ground floor structure from which you construct your life.

Those physical bodies you see everywhere about you, sustaining themselves with air, water, and food, emoting, thinking and sleeping, they're *illusions*, temporary vehicles fitting the soul for physical plane experience. They are not *real*. Most people only see this when loved ones are cold corpses in front of them. You know it *now*. What you see is the spark of divinity within, ever seeking knowledge and understanding, the soul seeing through the eyes and reaching out, through the heart and the hand, to touch and embrace. And that is what you relate to, with an empathy and sensitivity that reaches through the issues of the ego and the awkwardness of the personality to the Godly mission beneath. You are dealing with the divinity within, however deeply buried beneath the veils of denial and disbelief. You reach in, with your measure of divinity, and connect with theirs.

5

ANTAHKARANA

Connecting divinity with divinity through the dense denial of Earth vibrations is pretty much what is done when linking up with Higher Self. The medium of the connection is what the 'traditional' teachings, as exemplified by Alice Bailey, would call the antahkarana, the column of light reaching up from your crown chakra, through all the levels, to the formless worlds of light where Monads dwell. When that connection is cemented, through the daily embrace we call practice, little can harm its effectiveness. It is the God connection, the direct line to as much omniscience as your little brain can handle. And by that I mean not only capacity but actual firmly entrenched linguistic concepts that can be utilised to download the intelligence you seek. Otherwise you are limited to the sort of elusively brief mystical experience undergone by birthing mothers, near-death experiencers, and samadhi seekers: an intense yet indecipherable illumination followed by vague notions of a cosmic at-oneness. Wildly inspiring and reassuring, yes, but effectively communicable all too rarely.

And there are those who would say it cannot and should not be communicated, that any attempt would be tantamount to profaning the sublime. But I would argue that is old, outdated theology, and not fit for the ascension process we and the planet are undergoing. Exactly how much of the ancient wisdom we can hold in our minds and communicate to others depends, I believe, on our openness and our willingness to embrace the unknown, the mystifying, and the apparently inexplicable. If, for example, sub-atomic particles can be in two places at once or manifest different aspects depending on how they are observed, then so can we. For beings in the universe much greater than us, *we* are the sub-atomic particles, magically appearing and disappearing, *we* are the discrete packets of information defying repeated analysis. It's not just the alien Grays who find us bizarrely unpredictable and shockingly spontaneous.

Back to the antahkarana, that highway to Higher Self/Monad. Created long before birth by Monad's intention and strengthened by our knowledge and repeated intention, it slowly becomes an unshakable column of light between the poles of "little me" and "big me". An information highway with traffic flowing freely both ways. Big me, Monad, is viewing and absorbing your life information, and storing it away, along with all the other 'bits' of information from all its other lives. Just tonight in meditation, 'my' Monad reaffirmed that it is viewing 'Gordon's' life through my eyes, and that my attempts to consciously merge, although always welcome, are in some way superfluous, as my thoughts/emotions/experiences are almost constantly being communicated (vibrationally? energetically?) along the antahkarana. Really the project should be 'Gordon' opening up more and more to the life of the Monad. The information is there, travelling along the column of light and being subconsciously absorbed. The project is to make it conscious. Just *how* conscious remains to be seen.

MONAD: HISTORY OF THE INSTANT

Readers of *More Adventures In Eternity* will be familiar with Higher Self/Monad's perceptions and attitude. Higher Self (HS) joined that narrative specifically to raise the reader's (and 'Gordon's') comfort level with the notion of a "source self" – Jane Robert's term – from which little selves spring. This time around we're going to be submerged in HS's world-experience/reality-tunnel/angelic dream-life. This will be experiential reality as HS's sees and feels it in the moment-to-moment energy field in which he moves and has her being.

Right now, on this Tuesday morning in November of 2005, I hear that I am not to be so despairing of ever being able to translate HS's experience into language suitably supple and expansive in communicating his reality. It is quite possible, I am told, and actually should not be a problem for a writer of my talents and experience; that this is why "Gordon" was chosen for the task. *Was I picked or did I volunteer? Both, depending on which level of your being answers the question.* Somehow, that exchange seems indicative of how things are going to go.

HS: I do not recall 'coming into being', it would seem that I 'always was'. It is common amongst us, the cosmic clowns of the Monadic plane, to say we are drops of divinity in an ocean of divinity, or sparks of light in a sea of light. En masse we make up the body of God. Perhaps we are not beyond counting, but I have yet to encounter one who really cares enough to undertake the task. We are parts of the whole just as you are. Together you make up humanity, together we make up God. And just as humanity does not actually speak with one voice, nor does God. When you as individuals speak with whom you assume is God, you are actually talking with your Higher Self. It's as if a pet dog, in communing with its master, felt as if it were dialoging with humanity, when actually it is dialoging with a member of humanity.

You are to us as we are to God. *As above, so below.* So when you are 'chatting with the deity', as the intellectual cynics in your culture would have it, you are really chatting with a representative member of God.

We speak; when asked, we utter thought-concepts in response to your queries; God does not. Not to put too fine a point on it, *God is.* You can say the *is-ness* of everything, the aliveness of all forms, the sub-atomic structure of all creation, the silent submission of all life to the ongoing process of growth and decay; you can say all this and more, but essentially *God is.* The best way, and indeed the *only* way to talk with God is to merge with his/her being. Suspend the importance of your individuality and viewpoint, put all your issues in your back pocket and just *be a breathing being.* Then listen and feel as the universe vibrates around you. This will show you why dialoging with the deity is not only not possible in the conventional sense; it is also not needed.

To be omnipresent and omniscient is more than enough. The joy of being everything and everywhere, with all the energetic impulses endlessly coming and going from creator through created and back again is the thrill of all thrills and requires no commentary. Such ultimate vitality is all. To talk with God, you request one of the representatives, i.e., me or someone like me, and we do our best to come to your level; to experience God, you must, as an incarnate individual, open your heart and your head and feel. Feel the life all about you and beyond you, see how it endlessly intermingles, harmonies and discords constantly appearing and dissipating, all the striving and relaxing, all the desire expressing itself, and know that it is all God.

There are of course, many belief systems extant in your world which insist that many beings and attributes are not of God at all but are emanations of, or are perverted by, dark, demonic forces of one label or another. For us Monads, repositories of the vast majority of human/sentient experience on Earth throughout history as we are, this is just not so. We are hotels, as Gordon once put it, for good and bad guys alike. Victims, victors, the handsome the ugly, the smart the stupid; it's all the same to us as we head toward a totality of experience upon this unique planetary experiment.

To expand upon this, let me explain that every natural form on your planet is ensouled, not just humans and animals, but the forms of nature also; rivers, mountains, trees and so on. The same energy that ensouls a human has earlier (in your terms) ensouled rivers and mountains. That energy is, simply, our energy projected. In the last fifty or so years many incarnate humans have felt memories surfacing, not only of past human lives, but lives where 'they' seem to have been animals or trees or mountains.

Although yet confined to a vanguard of adventurous souls, this knowledge is more or less 'true'. So think of your energy, or part of your energy, ensouling a volcano. Think of the periodic eruptions and the damage and suffering they caused. Could you do anything about it? Could you alter your essential God-given nature? Think of when your energy ensouled a wolf or an eagle. You killed to survive. But you were also devoted to your mate, your pack and your offspring. Think of your primitive, tribal lives in the forests and mountains. You fought to avoid being killed, you killed to eat; you sacrificed to your notion of Gods who needed propitiation. In all these experiences, the so-called good was mixed with the so-called bad. We, as Monads, absorb it all, and absorb it gladly. It's all fuel for the fire of knowledge and wisdom. We are all becoming planets of dignity and wisdom, and you and all the ensouled forms of life are contributing to that goal and always have, whether you knew it or not.

When you and we graduate from this Earth, as fully-fledged planets of wisdom-experience, we will be more than able to ensoul distant stars slated to become planets for evolving life forms. We will become that planet's hierarchy of advanced souls who monitor and shepherd the evolutionary plan, just as advanced souls (called variously the white lodge, the ascended masters, the secret chiefs, the elder brothers) do so on Earth.

And that, in a nutshell of not very many words, is the essence of the divine plan or ancient wisdom. This is the truth passed in deep seclusion in many secret societies throughout history, the truth that the masses were rarely allowed to hear. That you are not just a body, a soul, an agent of the crown, a slave to the master, a sweating cog in the economy, a serf to the aristocracy, a servant of God, a pawn of religion, a provider of arms and children, an athlete, a trader, or a dancer, but only light, the idea of light, the emanation of light, a formless intelligence that loves to play, play in the fields of the Lord, and that is the ultimate piece of subversive information, the one that no family, society, hierarchical structure, religious, political or economic, wants you to know, for they need you where they've got you, subservient and obedient. Remember, *Let there be light? Well, that light was us.* And let me add, the forces which kept this divine freedom from the poor humans under their thumb, although acting from the selfishness of deep fear and the desire to retain power at all costs, served the evolutionary path well, for many of the souls incarnate during those times were far from ready to accept their ultimate cosmic freedom. They were afraid of the challenge and responsibility, and wished for the chains which bound them. Societal structures and religious threats kept young souls where they felt most comfortable, in the bosom of the seasons and the bondage of duty. And those same structures provided the rebellious and adventurous with hurdles to overcome and prisons to escape. Hungry, tired, and fearful peasants do not care to hear that they are as light *and* as free. They want more meat, more wine, more holidays, fancier cars, bigger houses. They want to serve a king, a country, a God, a fine raft of ideals; not be slaves to them.

That the revelation alluded to above is another initiation is perhaps obvious to the attentive reader. If souls are not quite ready for it, their attachment to their status and sense of importance and mission can sometimes cripple their progress. Everyone wants their lives, their strivings, to be meaningful in some way or other. To have them rendered meaningless through the revelation of cosmic insignificance can reduce the citizen to the perceived status of insect in no time flat. This crucifixion of self-importance is the great challenge of this initiation and I assume that most of you are ready to at least consider its implications if not yet undergo its rigors. Evolution of the soul on this planet can be seen as a growth and accumulation of talents followed by a gradual decay and divestment of attachments, leading back to a beginning with a new depth of understanding. You are always returning to where you once were with a new set of clothes, issues, and insights.

The crucifixion of self-importance is the stage you'll have to pass through on your may to merging with me, HS. For in that contact, you will be swamped with my light and vision and doubtlessly feel dwarfed by its measure of transcendence. You will also have to confront the others in the group soul, many of which have completed their fulfillment in incarnation. Even though they are beyond the need for homes, communities, and landscapes, and indeed all the functional challenges that life in the world of forms brings, they can spring to dimensional life any moment you express more than a flicker of interest, and their contribution to the mental/emotional/spiritual atmosphere of your incarnation will become quite apparent as the two of you exchange, usually ushering in greater and greater degrees of humility, until your ego appreciation has dwindled to zero or thereabouts. You are not particularly important, but your contribution to the whole certainly is. I, as HS, love all my incarnations equally, and not because it is a good operational management tool. You are not only my beloved children of light, *you are my light*. My light individualised and set free to explore, just as we Higher Selves are God's light individualised and set free to create. *As above, so below.*

The history of my instant, as Gordon has so cleverly put it, is one of rapid exfoliation. I am a tree whose roots and branches spread like wildfire, sprout leaves which bloom and fade, and contribute to a landscape of action and complexity. I am here and I am there. And like those sub-atomic particles you hear about, my positions change when they are illuminated by a focus of attention. When I am not actively examining, your forms and individual characters disappear. It's as if I exist in the dark, although it's not so much dark as empty, and have a huge bank of spotlights which I can trigger at will. Any one of these spots can illuminate a life form which my energetic impulse has vivified. I can suddenly see a river surrounded by trees, a wolf in a roaming pack, a villager rotting with the plague, a court jester grumbling in a corner, a child hiding in an attic afraid, a philosopher probing the deep meaning of fear, a rich woman dying in childbirth and a poor woman being handed an orphan, a duke being butchered in a sudden revolt, a thief double-crossing his colleagues for the cash, a priest in doubt preaching, a magician in power gloating, a peasant toiling in semi-barren fields, a fisherman overjoyed at a huge catch, lovers entwined and love denied. I feel the tiny creatures of the forest, frantic with fear, then full bellied and sleeping. Ancient trees in the desert, tiny sprigs in the meadow.

All this can occur in what you humans consider simultaneous time. But as I exist where time is not, it does not seem that way to me. I merely observe and receive the signals from "there". Of course my energies go out towards you all continuously, but this is rarely perceived, such is the complexity of energetic impulses that you exist in. Some of you may feel blessed by God, protected by a saint, inspired by an angel, guided by a good spirit, or maybe helped by the local witch/shaman figure. Such is the confusion of physical plane belief systems on your dense planet that only a few know the how and why of the Higher Self. Although the soul is most often given its due as a hidden source, one's original nature or gift of God, most tie themselves to intermediaries, the priests, the shamans, the guides, the angels, the prophets. The idea that the individual can communicate directly with her inner divinity entirely without the intercession of a self-appointed elite is limited to those souls who have not been overwhelmed by the 'organised' in religion.

Gordon is saying to me that there are many on Earth who would argue that man's natural laziness and timidity is actually the prime cause of the communication breakdown. To this I would say, yes, given the immense density chosen for this planet, challenging the incarnate souls with the greatest hurdle yet devised for maintaining active links to spirit, that is an originating factor, a factor that was originally coped with by the incarnation of more advanced souls who would become the tribal shaman figure, the one with conscious communication abilities to spirit. The priestly castes which gathered around the inevitable organising principle generated by the love of power and status merely took advantage of the individual's need for direction, and instead of encouraging those who fell short of the courage necessary, usurped their heritage and made them pay for the privilege.

Of course, there is a counter argument to this, which involves the acknowledgment of gross misuse of psychic powers during the long fall from grace of the Atlantean civilisation and the resultant necessity of priestly bureaucracies to reign in and redirect such self-centred, indulgent anarchy. A necessary evil some will say, to use your limiting Earth terminology for a moment. But again it could be added, with the inevitable dualism encountered on the physical plane, that the usual pendulum swing of energy caused an overlong repression of individual spiritual impulse which is only now being corrected, mainly by the efforts of those adepts and masters who would rather encourage such movements than further debate the cause of the logjam. Monads, you might have guessed, given our minor deity and impartial referee status, float above the rough seas of such debate, unable and unwilling to take sides. For us the outcome is as unavoidable as the endlessness of eternity. We champion no argument or movement, preferring to welcome the cut and thrust of debate, for the accumulation of competing viewpoints is pretty much what we're all about.

You might suppose we provide balance to paradox, argument and differing viewpoints, you might wonder if our level of bliss calms out the rivals and enemies. Both are partially correct; but what needs to be emphasised is that the post-mortem journey through the planes of spirit, with each level "burning off" the energies of desire and divisiveness and allowing the divinity within to gradually emerge through the veils, is actually how the balance is achieved. The energy for argument, rivalry, and vilification has been completely depleted by the time souls arrive "back here". If you, as an individual, are still burning with the passions, resentments, or competitive agendas of political, economic, or religious systems, not to mention their more personalized counterparts, you will be held at the astral level for which the working out and dissipation of such energies is appropriate. Simply put, you cannot get to where we are with that kind of baggage. Sometimes, if their hold on the individual has waned sufficiently, they can be put aside and left for later retrieval for the purposes of a quick visit. And when those brief initial merges with HS are achieved, much as Gordon has earlier detailed, the baggage cannot remain intact; it is worn away, smoothed out, diluted. You could also say it is leavened by bliss and objectified by distance. Highly detailed attitudes and elaborately tooled prejudices are revealed in their intellectual mediocrity. Clever defences stand naked in their mechanisms. Egos crumble for lack of validity. Without those veils the soul reassumes its original radiance and merges, however briefly, with its source.

When I send out a spark of my essence I am experimenting and exploring, combining and recombining energies to create a completely unique expression in the territories of time and space. For although it will be subjected to the rigors of the gene pool into which it is finally inserted and be subjected to the traits and tendencies so determined, its unique nature will never be fully compromised by genetic inheritance. The soul energy, which is, essentially, my contribution, will always assert its independence from even the most overwhelming of environmental factors. This streak of stubborn individuality is what makes humans stand out from other planetary based life forms and guarantees Monads like me enormous freedom in concocting our contributions.

It has always been a wild ride on Earth, from the heights of Atlantis to the depths of the Middle Ages, and humanity has benefited from the harshest incarnational regimen yet devised. When you, and we, graduate, we will be unbeatable. And perhaps we will ensoul a new species and series of civilisations on a planet not yet cool enough to support the extravagant terms of our design.

And that, really, is the ultimate game of life: devising new species and the planetary conditions to challenge them. Nature thrives, forms adapt, and species evolve. We are the intelligent designers, the finished product, the evolutionary pinnacle. In a very subtle and elaborate fashion, we are entertaining ourselves in the worlds of form. Because, as totally enlightened beings, minor deities morphing into planetary intelligences and back again, we require some interesting and diverting creative activity when we step out of the bliss of non-being. Stars, planets, and sentient civilisations floating suspended in the vastness of interstellar space are as interesting a challenge as anyone could devise. At least we think so.

And I put it in such a light-hearted way because Gordon tells me that many souls, although evolving to a deeper understanding of spirit and its evolutionary journey, still need to be reminded that all those achievements of intellect, spirit, social and economic organisation that they have spent centuries pushing for, are but preliminary exercises preceding graduation. They feel, as almost all mature souls do, that they will be resting on the laurels of their cultural achievements in a sophisticated heaven, custom tooled for their type. And while there are, in the heaven worlds, grand institutions along the lines of universities and temples where such achievements are exalted and celebrated and even greater plans constantly ruminated upon by the long and recently dead, the great leap is still of the beloved *form* into the long-forgotten *formless*, where everything cherished is instantly relinquished in the surrender to the bliss of non-being.

That final surrender of self-importance, that crucifixion of ego and soul and all their carefully nurtured attributes, is, of course, merely a blending of the little 'I' with the big 'I', in which nothing is lost and everything gained, but it sure doesn't look like that to the soul still mired in pride of accomplishment.

When we Monads send out our beloved explorers into the antipodes of consciousness we know that many of you will become so enmeshed in the depths of physicality and the charge of excited desire that is the reincarnation cycle – not to mention the almost innumerable belief systems concocted by various individuals and groups trying to make some kind of sense of the hardship and suffering of the physical plane – that you will not only quickly lose track of home base and its inherent divinity but also soon deny any trace of that quality in yourselves. That you can cycle through the physical and astral worlds chasing your tail, as the saying goes, is a recognised and inherent risk. In fact it was built into the design from the beginning. You are free to traverse the worlds of form for as long as your illusion sustains your desire to penetrate it.

We are content to wait while you become caught in the attractive traps of honour, pride, and achievement, of religious devotion and tribal loyalty. We are content because we have so much else to focus on, so many divine sparks ensouling forms of one type or another, that even a large group being "lost" in the folds of illusion for centuries can easily be coped with. Lost in hell, lost on Earth, lost in Heaven, it's all the same to us. We're interested in how you cope, your strategies and how you develop them.

When you begin to see that your religion is no more right than anyone else's and your tribe no more righteous than another, then you are on the long and winding road back to us. Power and status on Earth, born of deprivation and pain, pleasure and fulfillment in your choice of Paradise, prolonged punishment in the dark valleys of hell, hard won redemption and devoted service, all are the perfected mirrors of illusion, crafted by infinitely clever and creative desire. The radiant light lies outside these incriminating adventures, patiently awaiting your re-entry. And like a giant party, only those at the door will notice you have come back in. The general swell of good humour and hilarity will soon absorb you, and you will be happy to join the fun. Losing yourself in those vibrations is why you came in from the cold of your separated life. This you know as you remove your coat and your clinging and whining.

Gordon says he likes this metaphor but wonders if it doesn't mislead the reader. After all it is the bliss of non-being is it not? Well, let me compare it to taking an after-lunch nap. Both the napper and the soul exiting incarnation for the eternal bliss of non-being know that the world will still be going on in all its complex interactions and that they will not be missed. They are both happy to check out and feel that the upcoming rest is their due. They have both tired of action and feel that as much as possible has been accomplished with the energy available. And they both know that they will, as you say on Earth, live to fight another day. Perhaps the only difference is that the napper will awaken refreshed and ready to resume their life, and the soul returning from the light will arrive recharged as someone else. The beginning of someone new.

7

LIVING THE HIGHER-SELF CONSCIOUSNESS

Perhaps a word or two from Gordon about how he feels the consciousness of Higher Self/Monad is in his day to day life:

I feel as though I can ignore it most of the time and be this limited fallible human – subject to weather, hunger, and fluctuating moods. But it repeatedly butts in on my self-limitation at odd and sometimes inconvenient intervals and widens my view to, not just one, but several horizons, usually simultaneously, which of course, can be quite dizzying. There's all that history stuff, with all its important stages and movements, empires, and civilisations, and all those imperious personages looking like dolls' houses, little tin soldiers and temper tantrums. There's society shaking free from sleep and launching into the daylight hours, propelled by their needs, fears, and desires. There are the planes of form, all of them with souls coated in various bodies, working through the energies of their issues, whether reaping bitter fruit in a hell, enraptured with devotion in a heavenly landscape dedicated to some deity, or happily participating in the pleasures of a Paradise.

There is the radiant light of eternity, surrounding all the activity as sparks of divinity slide in and out of form, becoming an individual or becoming another nothing in the ocean of God-light. There are all the answers to all the knotty metaphysical questions, kind of dangling in the air like many plumed birds. There's the knowing that the quality we call 'God' lives in everything and everyone and that forms are merely the vehicles of our transit in this world. There's the socialising, the enmities, the celebrations, the suffering. There's the babies being born and the old, the sick and the dying. There's the famine, there's the plague, there's the war. There's the sun, that huge house of nutritional light, and the clouds that obscure it. There is Gordon, civility incarnate in this coffee shop, acting as though this enlightenment were just another thought. And wondering if the word of gord is also the word of God.

I look upon it all and say, 'let there be more light', and there is, but maybe only for me. And then of course, the bodhisattva thing, let it be for others as it is for me, on Earth as it is in heaven. Let me commit to the enlightenment of all sentient beings. Today anyway. Then I pack up my laptop and make for the door, on the road to other engagements of a more human nature. And sometimes Higher Self consciousness creeps in as I'm making my way to those engagements and I become again that being peering into many dimensions and wondering if these 'leaks' from other levels are a fair representation of Higher Self consciousness or merely all that I can cope with right now. It certainly does not seem to seriously affect my traffic navigation skills, whether I'm walking or driving. There's some sort of automatic pilot function that seems to kick in and manage just fine with only the ghost of Gordon at the helm.

The result of these repeated experiences is perhaps more subtle than obvious. The enlightenment does not flatten me with its profundity, or 'knock me for six' as some describe a shock; it does not even leave me as charmed as those shots of satori did years ago, when my immersion in Zen seemed an almost daily preoccupation. Perhaps multi-dimensionality is courting me with the collusion of calmness, as excitement seems the farthest thing from the experience. As I fumble to explicate this seeming conundrum, my inner guidance says this: "Excitement is of the astral body, and as you are experiencing this in your buddhic body, and using the antahkarana to bring it 'down and in', such agitations are not necessary or even desirable".

To continue, the calmness induced by these repeated incursions of multi-dimensionality into Gordon's daily experience feels like an acceptance, an absorbing of the next plateau, a recognition that, although wild and crazy, or even verging on insanity by the average person's standards, it is but another stage on Gordon's inner journey, and that many have already taken this path and crossed these thresholds. It is also a feeling that Gordon must be comfortable with this plateau before further unfolding can take place. Accompanying this is a sense that nothing on Earth really matters, that all experience is, as we say, grist for the mill, that all the euphoria, anxiety, and ballyhoo which accompanies political movements and 'natural' upheavals has now all the significance of a million leaves madly flapping in a summer storm. The cares of the country and the coercion of the headlines seem about as numerous and superfluous as the hair on the fur cap of the man who just walked below me.

The mystical journey has been called a selfish one, and I can see why. Even the basic parameters of the contemplative life can seem very self-serving to those bent on active intervention. But to underline, the distancing effect this multi-dimensionality has on Gordon does not seem to include a decline in compassion or sympathy. It's merely a recognition that the mass events of this plane have no more significance than, say, the adventures of a virus or a bacterium in the sub-atomic world or the arduous migrations of butterflies, birds, and fish, all of which takes place under our ignoring noses moment after moment, year after year. When you just have glimpses of the whole, the all in all, the ten thousand things dissolving into the one and then reforming instantaneously, you see that all of life, from the micro to the macro, is equally significant, and that none has priority over another, no matter how any species happens to rate itself. You are seeing with God-vision and, in your brief sharing, you know what God knows: all is sentient manifestation, all is divine, all is embraced.

In explicating this Higher Self/God consciousness to friends, clients and associates, one quickly finds it necessary to remain humble as well as civil, such is the potential for misunderstanding. As most folk are still holding their understanding at the physical/astral level, their concerns are physical and emotional. Even those of a strong spiritual bent stay focused on the astral plane euphoria of Paradise as the goal of their strivings. Few of these wish to hear that Heaven, as conventionally conceived, is an illusion catering to the desires of the emotional body. Nor do they wish to hear suffering, either individual or large scale, seemingly glossed over. The notion espoused by the famous line 'every man's death diminishes me' still holds great sway over much of mankind. In actual fact, there is no need for any suffering or death to diminish *anyone, but as we as a species still insist on the limited consciousness of three dimensions, almost everyone feels it is virtuous to subscribe to its sentimental illusions; so much so, in fact, that it is accepted as part of human nature. Any attempt to put compassion and sympathy in their proper place always skirts the dangerous territory taken by the fascists.*

Proper use of compassion is not the absence of compassion, it is merely the recognition that compassion intelligently directed can be much more effective than the self-indulgent wallowing in pity which is too often its usual expression. Certainly any random or planned act of kindness is welcome in our troubled world, and indeed a plague of that quality in action would work wonders, but the Higher Self/God consciousness recognises that all suffering is karmically bonded, although the multidimensional interactions of actions and consequences is infinitely more complex than the standard notions of cause and effect/ sowing and reaping.

In discussing this, I am repeatedly reminded of various tales about beings like Sai Baba who are easily able to envision karmic causes of personal difficulties and disease as they stand, either physically or psychically, in front of the soul requesting assistance. Even more run of the mill aspirants and psychics (like myself) have shades of this experience and I have more than a suspicion that the ability will increase and be refined in us all. How one moves from being an ordinary psychic to the enlightenment of a Sai Baba is an enigmatic challenge so far bereft of suitable description but I know it's a path that 'Gordon' is on. How he accumulates the confidence and discernment necessary will likely be a great source of fascination for years to come. Meanwhile I observe his every move with an interest bordering on delight.

8

THE CAST OF CHARACTERS

During my years of past life regressions, spontaneous recollections, lucid dreaming, meditations and recollected out of body experiences, I have come across many once incarnate personalities with whom I appear to share a group identity, that of Higher Self/Monad. Now seems like a good time for a listing of the leading players. They are all individuals acting their parts in the history of their families/societies, but the more I examine their lives the more they feel like archetypes of human behaviour, as if they were an extended exercise in amalgamating attributes into various experimental concoctions, like a chef practicing for the perfect banquet to top off her career. These experiments in character formation, while deserving of all the respect and dignity accorded the average citizen in a democratic state, become, as they are carefully considered, more like the members of a collective, tailoring their personal aims for the common goal of creating the ultimate well rounded character, balanced in all ways, and fit to be an all-understanding, all-embracing creator deity elsewhere. Of course during their earthly careers, only a few of them realised this goal, and those only in fleeting moments of inspiration or crisis. Mostly they struggled with their mortality and the social and economic issues of their lives. The daily grind of doing one's duty according to the norms laid down in that epoch and society.

The following scenario, detailed by Higher Self and transmitted through Gordon, will hopefully elaborate on the hints and notions earlier given out on this series, and expand on the simple ideas of cause and effect that are the result of seeing a linear development throughout history of past lives, of which you, the examiner, are the latest development.

Gordon, "I", whom you know:

1. A king, circa 1570-1630
2. A philosopher, circa 1700-1770
3. Another philosopher, 1300's
4. A druid priest figure, circa 20 B.C. - 30 A.D.
5. A Celtic chieftain of the middle ages
6. A small time businessman in ancient China
7. A wife and mother in ancient China
8. A trader in Holland, circa 1600-1650
9. A young girl, dead at around five, circa 1900
10. An outcast, selling herself to survive, England circa 1730
11. A wife awaiting the return of her husband from sea
12. A wealthy and influential Venetian courtesan, circa 1550
13. A member of the priestly caste under Ahkenaten in Egypt
14. An artistically inclined son of a wealthy Athenian family, bisexual
15. A lesser known member of the Neoplatonist school
16. A contemplative monk in England, circa 1300
17. An abbot of a monastery, circa 1400
18. An Irish monk, circa 700
19. A daughter of high birth, left pregnant while husband goes to war, 1650
20. Also an archetype for 11, young wife who lost her husband at sea, circa 1880
21. A French noblewoman with an inherited estate, bisexual playgirl, circa 1780
22. An Atlantean male, steeped in magical energy work, yet carefree and completely without the ego attachments of those who engaged in the 'magical workings' of more recent times
23/24. A woman and a man, fairly primitive, brutal 'Viking Raider' types

25. Minor Scottish noble, impoverished, circa 1250
26. Buddhist monk (India/Tibet/Nepal) circa 1000

The above characters are only a representative sample, the most influential, and if you like, habit-forming creatures in the available spectrum. As my grasp on Higher Self reality is as yet incomplete, perhaps I would be wise to say 'the most influential on Gordon'. I certainly feel their repeated influence on Gordon's issues and choices, and I believe my psychic influence on them is something that will come up as we continue to explore. All the Higher Self projections put together might look like a mini-society, with every character type and ethnic trait represented. What I think you're getting here is a small clan within that group.

The following will be Higher Self's perceptions filtered through Gordon's partial understanding and 20th century English verbal conceptualisations. Gordon is convinced that the result will fall far short of what is desired for the project, but Higher Self feels that even an approximation will be a significant step forward in human understanding, and thus well worth the effort.

Higher Self: When the call went out for volunteers to populate the new planet with sentient life forms, the more curious and adventurous among us made our way to the solar system to peruse the intriguing possibilities. Incarnating with conviction on such an incredibly dense material plane, such as then existed on the surface, was considered an almost worthless exercise in not much more than vanity. Of course, populating a planet with bits of yourself, however divine, could be seen as the quintessential vanity project anyway, but adding stupidity to the brew failed to lend any enchantment to the challenge for most of us. We compromised by sending energy beams down as far as the astral levels and working on the civilisation that became known, mythologically at least, as Lemuria, or Mu. The humanoid life forms thus created experienced no disconnection, as you currently understand it, from soul and divine purpose. Doubt, agonising indecision, frustration and anger were virtually unknown to these proud and noble creations, and the astral Paradises they happily created and inhabited exist to this day as the astral heavens of many ethnic persuasions. In a way, building your own afterlife before first incarnating was an interesting innovation. Certainly, when the physical plane was ready for human habitation, it was only ready for the roughest and shortest of lives.

Some of us were experienced life creators and some of us were new-bies. The units of divine energy called Monads are well able to wander the created universes without actually becoming involved in the incarnation game. The path to planet maker is an option not a requirement. Manipulating the basic units of energy to produce matter of varying grades and construct all the rock, soil, water and plant life is a task for the deeply experienced creator Monads, something a lot of us were not at that point. Enthusiastic wannabes would be more accurate. Am I asking you, the reader, to believe that millions of us Monads zip around the manifested universe, as massless and enigmatic as photons, just looking for something interesting to do? Pretty much. God's spitting us out from his/her limitless being on a fairly regular basis, and although we're welcome to hum along in the ocean of blissful light, almost as omniscient and omnipresent as the grand old man himself, we're also free to slip out into manifestation and see how the game is played there. With one step we're out in the worlds upon worlds, and with another we're back in the radiant emptiness inside. Like that thing you do down there, umm...breathing.

Back to Lemuria: when we were shown how evolution was intended to unfold on the Earth, at least the basic game plan anyway, we were a little less reluctant to fully engage. The dense and primitive conditions were slated to evolve into something more conducive to culture and creativity. At first we'd have to be content with attaching sharpened stone to the end of a stick, gathering berries and nuts, and the simple luxuries of caves in the rainforest to protect our charges from the hungry predators that were also in our care, but the contrast, through the magic mirror of time, to Ernest the bank manager, puttering about in his potting shed with grafts and orchids before feeding his rabbits and walking his Samoyed, was too tempting. And the hundreds of thousands of years in between, with all their ups and downs, achievements and setbacks, would, in your terms, make the meat of the sandwich.

Linear time and free will: yes, I hear you. Linear time and its relative reality is definitely an issue for Gordon. He can't, he tells me, reconcile the model of successive rebirths as revealed by the modern practice of past life regression with its current understanding of my incarnation/creation activities, which seems virtually simultaneous and leaves no room for such concepts as consequence, education and what he calls 'recombining of basic elements to make a better model'. My answer would be this, the human examining his rebirths is subject to the laws of time, which although applying only to the physical plane,

are nevertheless real, and result in such things as action and consequence and the educative spiral sometimes called evolution, while I,
outside the dictates of his and her story, with all its pathos, humour,
and conflict resolution, am completely free to examine the so-called
progress at any stage of the action. By which I mean, I can stop time,
make reassessments and decide on fresh initiatives. Gordon asks, "How
can the 20th century model improve on the 8th if they and all the others are 'created' in the same space of no-time? The two metaphors of
multidimensionality and the spotlights in the darkness would again
be helpful here.

On one level of my multidimensional nature, I manifest all the energy beams that will travel 'down' through the planes towards incarnation. Like streaks of light in your night sky they race towards their
destinations, gathering the various bodies they need for the task on the
way. Observed and assisted by various angelic beings who have moved
up through the ranks and are ready to render such delicate and precise
engineering, they acquire, in certain prescribed ratios, various packets
of energy from many vibration levels which result in personality characteristics and physical, mental, emotional, and spiritual 'tendencies'
that will react in the tempestuous physical plane, calling such ingredients as 'character', 'destiny', and 'luck' into being; not to mention manifesting qualities like 'determination', 'sloth', and 'terror'.

To detail all that these angelic beings fashion for the incarnation project would take a book in itself, but suffice to say that many
of the fleshy templates were pioneered in other planetary systems
and brought to Earth for appropriate retooling, and that the semi-
dormant chakra system in the etheric body is ready to spring into
action with the appropriate physical plane triggers. For example,
though you may not care to, you can certainly thank the dragons,
dinosaurs, and other massive predatory creatures with helping to
fashion your unfortunately still highly functioning first 'fight or
flight' chakra all those millennia ago. Some of you are already engaged in acts of semi-conscious gratefulness as you, perhaps unwill-
ingly, cooperate with the creatures you call the Reptilians, who are,
as some of you have doubtlessly guessed, the 'species' who evolved
from those ancient creatures still dwelling in the dark recesses of
the human imagination. The Reptilians have refined third chakra
willfulness and determination into a power tool so automatically
effective that it prevents any higher part of their nature from manifesting but, as they align themselves with the power lust active in

humans, flattering themselves with fantasies of planetary control, they are also learning the heart chakra lessons that humans have so carefully nurtured throughout the centuries as they waged the passionate wars of their astral natures, crucifying themselves on issue after issue until all passion was finally spent and surrender to one's higher nature seemed like the only option still open.

To return to the point at hand, as I examine the 'progress' of one of 'my' souls by shining that energetic spotlight upon them, I can feel just what they are generating from their life experience and what will be useful in my data banks of sentient experience, and make what you might call the 'necessary adjustments' in another energetic probe. For example, a terror that produces cowering bereft of any courageousness will result in 'me' adjusting another soul's similar predilection, tilting it toward bravery in identical situations. Of course if I tilt too far I may get another monster of tyranny, whose courage has not been sufficiently leavened by mercy, and every possible permutation in between. Add to this all the cultural, societal, and familial influences on characters and you will glimpse what a complex playing field I am operating in. Not to mention that incarnate ego's resistance to 'my' influence. Because of belief systems I am often reduced to the 'good angel' of one's better nature and am thus susceptible to the inherent rebelliousness of the young ego in training. And for egos who become completely mired in the sheer physicality of their desires and fears, I am little more than a rumour or legend, or in your modern terms, a compensatory fantasy.

As already mentioned, I can stop time for these deliberations and adjustments, just as many of you can do in your between-life musings in the spirit planes. Of course I see that this would seem impossible or at least magical for many incarnate souls but it is, I assure you, a 'fact' of 'my' existence. And as useful a tool as it may be, it is far from being perfected and, due to the pre-eminence of free will on Earth, I doubt it ever will be.

I, like almost any Monad, can tell you of how I am currently struggling with the overweening pride of this soul, the slothfulness of that soul, and the wildly neurotic tendencies of a third, not to mention the paralysing fears, overwhelming lusts, and controlling thirsts of many others. Throw in a fair measure of timidity, conformity, and life-limiting choices and you have got a fair grab-bag of our daily diversions. Not that we experience days, but you know what I mean. And every Monad has a number of soul probes caught in the physical-astral reincarnation cycle controlled by tribes and religions.

Those plague victims dead in babyhood, those children fighting and dying in ethnic wars, those repeatedly resorting to the daily dependence of opiates and alcohol, those who repeat their religious or tribal belief system, life after life, frustrated but safe in the bondage of their simple constructions; they all originate from us. Of course, we all have our high achievers as well: the philosophers, the scientists, the entrepreneurs and industrialists, the devoted homemakers who ensure the loving education of several striving souls. And as you can no doubt see, we need them all, the slow pokes, the high flyers, and every shade in between, to contribute to our expansion and eventual graduation.

As well as my influence and meddling(!) all you soul probes influence each other. There are invisible lines of energy running amongst and between all of you. You are endlessly broadcasting the details of your experience to the others, who are in turn, sending their information back to you. In most cases this exchange is entirely sub-conscious, and your guess that its growth throughout the millennia has built what you moderns have come to see as the archetypes and behaviour patterns of the racial unconscious. Soul probes, in their various epochs, societies and daily lives, have slowly constructed the entire repertoire of actions, attitudes and reactions – the behavioural gene pool you might say – from which every incarnate human can, and does, draw.

If this conflagration of unconscious communication seems overwhelming, then let it be understood that every human has their predilection for choosing from a certain and usually quite narrow waveband of information. The proud and arrogant will have their preferred area of choice, as will the pious, the timid, the rebels, the willfully criminal, the conventionally ambitious. To use your modern life metaphor, everyone has their favourite radio stations that they turn on day after day. So there you have it, subconscious behavior and motivation radio. Let me at least outline how I, the Monad, experience it.

Just as a nameless, characterless wave of energy, rolling around without form or intention in that sea of light some call the Godhead, shoots out into the world of form and becomes a manifested unit of energy, a Monad, beams of energy suddenly become active within me, shoot out into manifestation, dropping like anchors through the various levels of spirit and finally coming to rest in the mud of the physical plane as a fetus in a womb. Do 'I' manifest these beams from a base of desire or do 'they' manifest themselves without my conscious bidding? The answer, perhaps maddeningly for the more rational among you, is both. Both and more.

As I move you further into my multidimensional territory you will be asked repeatedly to see the answers to your perhaps unspoken but nevertheless *felt* questions as operating on *several levels simultaneously*. The only thing that is straightforward out here is the fact that nothing is straightforward. Answers are always multiple, and plumping for a favourite, inadvisable. To see all answers as merely responses in the ongoing flux and reflux in the flight paths of energised forms, 'optional journeys to further option-producing entanglements' is something of the complex flavour I wish to impart. Passing out from the One to the Many is the universal breathing pattern, *in and out forever,* and, whilst in the pause of the outbreath, we confront multiplicity. Ingrained belief and prejudice may precipitate a choice or choices, but sustained contemplation will reveal all choices as options and illusions. Despite the myths of science and its related belief structures, there is very little actual 'objectivity' in your world. In ours there is none. Multiplicity of perception is the sea we swim in. Joyfully, in case you're wondering. Maybe 'freedom from lack of joy' would be more accurate.

What I can tell you clearly is this: That sense of 'oceanic oneness', experienced by them all in their mother's womb, is a reflection of the 'oceanic oneness' of the radiant unmanifest, the void all a-bustle with endless invitation, the Godhead. Only now it is modified by the thoughts and emotions of each mother, which, as you can imagine, vary from bursting with maternal bliss although a tired 'oh-no-not-again' resentment to a resentful and perhaps angry 'how-can-I-get-rid-of-this-one?' game plan. This modification is the first serious impingement on any being's bliss. These all-too-human thoughts and emotions jab and irritate. As a preparation for the birth into that school of hard knocks, otherwise known as Earth, it is quite useful. Those irritations, as you all know, are going to continue no matter what.

9

IMAGINE

Imagine all my energy beams/soul probes flying away from my core simultaneously, just as all the Monads were ejected from the God-head simultaneously. It's the execution of creation on the altar of desire. The crucifixion of God as she discovers her tears, his joy and that journey of all journeys to those undiscovered countries of darkness and density where the answers to all questions cower before experience, craving penetration.

Imagine all these beams becoming conscious of themselves as somehow distinct, beings with boundaries, selves which sensed that there was, somewhere, a not-self, entities which knew their knowledge was slowly being narrowed and that limitation was something they now had to deal with. The limitless bliss that was their being now only beckoned from afar.

Imagine their sadness at being left behind, their dislocation, their anger, their angst. Imagine God's excitement: Hey, I've created something! What next? We're talking *no-universe* then *constantly-expanding-universe* here. No time or space then suddenly history, distance and objects interacting. Mass, gravity, attraction repulsion, and lots of stuff spinning about madly. No small thing, I think you'll agree.

Imagine all this fresh creation overcoming its cosmic loneliness and realising everything was multiplying like mad and that any chunk of creation could endlessly re-create at a whim. Imagine them singing:

Hey, we're Gods too! Imagine them shooting out bits of themselves, joyfully, like little kids learning to spit and whistle. Imagine almost no limits on this giddiness.

Imagine millennia passing as various experiments in creation unfold.

Imagine those millennia meaning nothing.

Imagine planets and photons and the endlessly reworked recipes that resulted in them.

Imagine unimaginably huge galaxies and the giant emptiness inside atoms. *Imagine* what fun it all was, and still is.

Imagine not giving what you would call 'a damn', about anything, ever, because there is nothing to expend 'care' upon. There is only the endless joy of 'creative' activity.

Imagine us as dying leaves in a fall breeze, spinning about giddily through something we would later call universes, helplessly creating as flowers bloom and produce fragrance.

Imagine an affidavit signed by God attesting to the veracity of this experience: you might as well as it is as close to proof as you're ever going to get. For in this realm of complete subjectivity, any version and interpretation is as valid as any other. There is no such thing as the truth, or the way it is, or was. There are as many truths as there are sentient perceivers to relay them. Your more courageous scientists in the realms of mathematics and physics are beginning to recognise this but keep themselves safe from ridicule by couching their suspicions in the private language of their discipline. For example, take the lifestyles of your average 'photon' or 'neutrino': the ultimate in go-anywhere do-anything vehicles for consciousness expression, breaking every rule and behaviour pattern. By separating the microcosmic from the macrocosmic, these scientist types can keep the frail sanity of human limitation intact. That humans can be as utterly free and without definition or limitation as these tiny 'particles' are safeguarded from mass consumption. But that is how we were and how you can be once you renounce all title to form, evolution and karma.

Imagine the marvelous complexity of creation, as we did, way back when in the history of instants, as our joy thickened into thought.

Imagine how nothing mattered but the new bliss of making. Madcap multidimensional production lines multiplying themselves into infinity. Thought-forms, ideas, energy structures, joyfully chaotic and lacking any definition that you would call useful. Beyond and beyond and beyond.

Gradually, of course, we explore the variability of vibration and slowly lower the rates, moving into conceptual territory such as density, gravity, and mass. At least that's what you call them now. Then we merely noted the manifestations and suspected one perceptible activity being consequent upon another. Eventually material resembling your notion of 'matter' made its presence felt.

When physical level matter is created now, usually on new planetary systems, it is practiced by apprentice devas and discarnate humans overseen by angelic beings deeply experienced in such activities, but 'back then' there were no such gradations of sentience. Hierarchies of spiritualised experience had yet to make their experience. We had seemingly manifested matter but as yet had no means of exploring it. Depending on how we, as Monads, regulated our own vibration, we would either pass through the appearance of solidity rather as a human ghost does now, or we wandered through the seemingly random chaos of sub-atomic activity like carefree photons. Mesmerising, entrancing, are the sort of terms you would use to describe the experience in the 'now' of your ongoing experience. We did not, of course, see that we were regulating or adjusting our vibration, we were still experimenting and playing. The whole notion of forms and the animating of them with the energy we now call soul or spirit was still an idea waiting to be charmed into conception.

Gordon is finding it difficult to imagine, never mind describe, the creation of planets from gaseous states and the arrival of landscape features where none had previously existed. Where was the blueprint for all this if nothing physical had previously existed? Although we Monads are something along the line of minor deities we are not the totality, the prime cause, or as some would have it, *All That Is*. Certain causes are veiled even from us. Some of us noticed an ability to move through that level we now call time and we noticed that solid looking spheres were beginning to make their presence felt. The principle of form evolving had yet to be understood so we did not quantify it that way.

Of course all this proceeded at a leisurely pace; those gaseous furnaces took a while to cool down. Meanwhile those of us who had explored the time dimension knew some fundamental changes were due: land and sea were becoming distinct and elementary life forms existed in both. Although the concepts 'angelic' and 'architect' were not exactly in use, we suspected such entities must be in some way responsible for what we could see. But who were they? We returned through the medium of time, not really knowing how or why it worked the way it did and settled to muddle through the possibilities. Further investigation suggested that these angelic architects were likely emanations from us, at a 'time' when such emanations became conceivable. Some of us travelled farther 'along' this medium and saw the elementary beginnings of aquatic, avian, and mammalian life. Human society came, as you say, 'later', and was of course, not at the physical but the astral level. They were more ideas of humanity than actual beings as you understand them now.

Much to our surprise other Monads appeared from, well, elsewhere, armed to the teeth with attitude and ideas. Wouldn't you know it, they'd already put together universes and had been invited here to help us out. Our far flung corner of the multi-verse now had some kind of definition; apparently we'd been parked in this area you now call the Milky Way while some senior technicians could be persuaded to beef up our team. Team? We didn't know anything about a team!

Now these senior Monads already had plenty of 'beings' incarnate on a variety of planets and other vibrationally defined areas of experimentation, so they wouldn't be developing any incarnational contacts, just showing us how to. And boy did they show us lots. Instead of joyously exploding in every direction at once we learned how to focus our giddy pleasures into purposeful lasers of creative intent. Disciplining our fun into something more like a finished product.

As we watched planets settle into the more stable forms of landscape features and passed back and forth through the transformation you would call time, we became more excited and involved, to the point where we could not disentangle ourselves from the system of endless activity. There was no 'turning inward', there was no escape; we were inextricably bound up in the process of creation. Sure we were being creative, but we were also being created. The more we did the more we became. The whirl of sub-atomic particles was fascinating to exist in; we were not merely observing or participating, we were *being*. And the more we embraced the many manifestations the greater we became. Eventually we saw that *nothing is not us*.

The travelling through time unfolded more and more with every venture. Forms evolved into other forms and something akin to subtlety or complexity always ensued. The senior Monads showed us how to ensoul the forms we had seemingly constructed. You humans see animate and inanimate, sentient and non-sentient, organic and inorganic, the plenum and the void; we understand various levels of energy, some more self-conscious than others and some more cosmically conscious then self-conscious. That knowing of the self, that consciousness, is the only reality. And the only illusion is the notion of limitation. There is nothing that we, or you, cannot know or be.

Imagine. Just *imagine.* That's all we did. And eventually, we embraced our irreversible entanglement, became the process and owned our activity.

10

ENOUGH

———◆———

That's enough, thinks Gordon, receiving the information. Enough for now anyway. He says his belief system, the remaining shreds of it anyway, is being strained. Can we do something more, well, human? Some details of the human drama perhaps? The stories of incarnation? Yes Gordon thinks, that's what we need.

Gordon thinks incarnation is the ultimate narrative, the story from which all stories devolve. From nothing blossoms something; a sentient entity experiences itself as participating in a series of environments and events from which attitudes and ideas develop. And these ideas and attitudes help to build the consensus realities you call societies and cultures. Of course they also help maintain them and their dictating facades that function as oppressive illusions for the evolving individual in the process of detaching and taking flight. And from Gordon's perspective that is an excellent model. For 'me' of course it is not enough. My reality, which is also Gordon's when he steps up to share it, is many, many stories unfolding simultaneously.

Inexplicable energetic impulses which seemingly emanate from within 'me', the deep mystery that is Monad, shoot forth to fly through the various levels of density/areas of vibration, accumulating the coatings which are recognised as 'bodies' and landing in one or other of the consensus realities to experience the energetic interactions which compose 'life' on that level eventually to reap the wisdom rewards afforded by those who have the capacity for such endurance. Forming lives on planets, whether on the physical or non-physical levels, is what I'm all about. Of course, that 'I' is made up of many 'I's', some of whom are still entwined in the incarnational process and some who have completed their journey, having passed through all the desirous expectations of their belief system, have come to rest in the giant blissful and beyond blissful nothingness that I am part of.

The 'I' that I am can observe the many little 'I's' at any stage of their evolvement, should I so choose. I cannot, however, control or direct; attempt to impress perhaps. Each soul is, ultimately, its own protagonist, director, and audience. And I only get maximum benefit when the individual entity has a belief system which includes something along the lines of a creator deity, or deities, to whom they direct their aspirations and anxieties. We do not demand supplication or sacrifice, and never did, it was merely the rigors of the physical plane and the rather low-level anthropomorphising of primitive societies which produced such manifestations. We knew our soul probes would lose their sense of divine connection in the darkness of Earth's density and low vibration – we just did not know to what extent – and, of course it turned out to be much more than we'd dare to suspect. Over the centuries, lower astral entities were gradually formed out of the resulting debased and distinctly un-pleasant vibrations of human anger, fear, and lust, and they, little more than collection point clouds of amorphous desire for blood, lust, and cruelty, responded to the need by impersonating/taking on the persona of a demanding, jealous deity. Bonds were thus formed which exist, in one form or another, to this day; that is this day in which the reader reads, and they exert the same magnetic pull on earthbound creatures caught in the hypnotic desires of the lower chakras: those to whom the kill-or-be-killed, win-before-you-lose, death-before-dishonour scenarios are all.

Such self-restricted souls are virtually beyond our reach, save the few shreds of true God worship which may have survived their long immersion in the hellish realms, and which can sometimes be effective in charming the dormant heart into action, although often that action will only encompass the blood ties of family and tribe.

Fortunately, if such a quality can accurately be applied to Higher Self reality, many of my soul probes retain belief systems which include guardian spirits, angelic figures and deities which appeal to the higher and more refined impulses in man, and those beliefs allow us, Monads, to impersonate the deities they wish us to be, or at the very least, adopt the channels of communication to those supposed deities for our own communications. In this we may sound similar to the previously mentioned lower astral entities bloated on the blood and lust sucking activities previously detailed, and one could cast our activity as the higher and lower versions of the same function. Certainly our version will aid the individual in evolving beyond their various self-sustaining illusions, whereas theirs keeps the ignorant adherent strapped into a dead-end exercise of barely more than mutual admiration.

11

A SAMPLING OF
SOUL PROBES

R eminder:

Gordon, "I", whom you know:

1. A king, circa 1570-1630
2. A philosopher, circa 1700-1770
3. Another philosopher, 1300's
4. A druid priest figure, circa 20 B.C. - 30 A.D.
5. A Celtic chieftain of the middle ages
6. A small time businessman in ancient China
7. A wife and mother in ancient China
8. A trader in Holland, circa 1600-1650
9. A young girl, dead at around five, circa 1900
10. An outcast, selling herself to survive, England circa 1730
11. A wife awaiting the return of her husband from sea
12. A wealthy and influential Venetian courtesan, circa 1550
13. A member of the priestly caste under Ahkenaten in Egypt
14. An artistically inclined son of a wealthy Athenian family, bisexual
15. A lesser-known member of the Neoplatonist school
16. A contemplative monk in England, circa 1300

17. An abbot of a monastery, circa 1400
18. An Irish monk, circa 700
19. A daughter of high birth, left pregnant while husband goes to war 1650?
20. Also an archetype for 11, young wife who lost her husband at sea, circa 1880.
21. A French noblewoman with an inherited estate, bisexual playgirl, circa 1780
22. An Atlantean male, steeped in magical energy work, yet carefree and completely without the ego attachments of those who engaged in the 'magical workings' of more recent times
23. & 24. A woman and a man, fairly primitive, brutal 'Viking Raider' types
25. Minor Scottish noble, impoverished, circa 1250
26. Buddhist monk (India/Tibet/Nepal) circa 1000

Let's take a peek in what you would call the 'right now' so you can feel the transcendence of time and space that is 'my' almost constant experience. I am feeding Gordon images and ideas: I am helping the king, (1), who has come through difficult and delicate negotiations with himself, what he perceives as 'God' and others, to decisions that will hopefully balance the various needs and desires of the warring religious communities under his care; I am feeding two male philosophers, (2) and (3), mental energy to assist in their cogitations (although I do not attempt to impose any type of result); I am giving courage to the lonely, fearful wife, (11), who fears she has lost her husband at sea; I am giving two courtesans, (12), and a colleague, the perceptive power they need to distinguish their appreciation of 'God' from their disgust of his selfish, grasping, power-addled servants on Earth, while trusting that same energy might be used to corral and redirect some of their own vanities; I am offering the energy of courage to a number of soul probes involved in dangerous, perhaps life-threatening circumstances, including expectant and delivering mothers in situations where the risk of infection is high and the availability of competent medical care low. Various spirit guides and angels are drawing their inspiration from me as they go about their nurturing and playful activities with adults and children; I am experiencing the incarnate 'feel' of mountains, trees, and rivers and their part in the overall ecology of their area; and finally, I observe the mosaic of energetic interactions between all my soul probes, as they feed and receive impulses from each other.

As the king, (1), worries about his wife, who has recently delivered but is still confined, the philosopher, (2), considers the more human aspects of the kingly life, about which he is writing; the poor discarded wretch, (10), made pregnant by her employer, wanders the fields and lanes of her rural territory, begging for a berth and some employment; the high born maiden, (19), romanced into her knight's father's castle, awaits his return with babe in belly, and the Dutch trader, (8), awaits with trepidation the birthing of his second child, and the ancient Chinese trader, (6), looks forward to child number six, while the contemplative monk, (16), simultaneously prays for the health and well-being of all the local children and gives thanks that he himself does not have to so cope, and the abbot, (17), prays for guidance and forgiveness concerning the pregnancy of a nun he is particularly close to. Of the three women left by their adventuring husbands, (11), prays that she might be miraculously, immaculately pregnant, (19), shivers in a cold castle and awaits her delivery, anxious about the future and her over-solicitous father-in-law, and, (20), just prays for the safe return of her beloved. As you can imagine, all their thoughts, anxieties, fears, joys, and prayers come in my general direction and as I absorb, reflect, and transmute, they become a small catalogue of possible reactions to an archetypal situation in human physical existence; and, as you're no doubt thinking, another contribution to my data banks of incarnate experience.

Now take that thought and apply it to, say, a simple expression, of, say, frustration or impatience. Each one of the above characters, because of their varying energetic makeup, have a distinct experience of that mode and thus express themselves uniquely, although each microsecond and tiny shade of difference is influenced by all the other personalities. Singly they contribute to their personal drama, but collectively embroider a many-hued pattern, a veritable encyclopedia of impatience, whose details can be drawn on in the later stages of my, and our, ascension.

When the king, (1), contemplates a decision of state, he draws upon not only his own decision-making abilities and the strength he draws in prayer from his 'God', but also all the decision-making abilities, and lack of, in all the others in his 'soul group', and, lest it not be apparent, his eventual magisterial announcement will influence the many more quotidian decisions of the monks, mothers, and sailors he shares his source with. Whether they know it or not, and most do not, each is of the other and gradually contribute their strengths and weaknesses to the advancement of the whole. Of those who do know, perhaps four might be mentioned: (4), (13), (16), and (22), all had distinct perceptions, whilst deep in prayer or contemplation/meditation, of other humans who seemed to share a love, a source, a harmony, a common bond, difficult and perhaps too subtle to elaborate on.

(4), a Druid from ancient Britain, and who speaks for two other personalities from that culture, would like to comment:

"I do not care whether I am identified by a number or not, as my attachment to that personality is diminished to an intellectual curiosity at best. I once was proud and expected the respect I automatically gave to others, but that has all melted into the bliss of being a leaf on a God-tree, feeling the divine vibrations as not just rippling through my being but making up the totality of my being. Non-stop ecstasy is my lifestyle of choice now. It's not something I care to draw apart from. When one sees that one's earthly efforts have not only reached complete fulfillment but have also come to naught, one is freed from the attachment to achievement, whether on the level of the personal, cultural, political, or religious. One understands that these projects and efforts are not only worthy but endlessly ongoing, and that there are many souls moving up through the ranks, as it were, who will soon be ready to contribute to the various causes, and that you, the one who retires his former vigour in favour of some mysteriously beckoning future on a dimension as yet unexplored, not only has no more to gain, but nothing to lose, and that the game is convened for those who need to play. You no longer need.

"The Druid project has borne fruit in many ways we barely suspected in what is now considered its heyday. Besides seeding many native shamanic cultures in ways which have now become so accepted as to be forgotten, it has adapted itself to your modern industrial, technological world. There are many modern Druids, and I would advise any of them who might chance upon this text that although many of us 'elders', as it were, are now retired in that 'bliss beyond understanding', our temporal selves, seemingly secluded in our ancient timespans, can still be contacted in meditation for whatever benefit the practitioners may feel they can accrue. Of course, our retired selves, journeys completed and fulfilled, can also be contacted by any who sense our current state and willingness, but it should be noted that what we can give is very much the same as that which many others from other traditions may give, as the divine voice speaks through us all without distinction or deference.

"For a system with its feet so firmly planted in the soil, I can now see it also had its roots in the sky, its Father in Heaven, as our would-be conquerors the Christians, would say. Devoted brotherhood with the spirits of nature in the various gardens that always were and always will be, Eden, despite the harsh lessons of the mother you now call Gaia, was devised in the divine imagination to clothe and accommodate the growth needs of, not only certain human souls, but also the nature spirits they would come to feel so close to. The Christian dispensation that I initially felt so inimical towards was designed with other stages of growth in mind. Essentially, as I now understand it, it was another attempt at the One God concept, tried and defeated in Egypt, now reformatted with a proper messiah and his retinue. All those squabbles now seem too quaint to the me that resides in the greater energy being/self with which you now seek to merge. I have rescued myself from the arguments of religion, manicured my remaining outstanding attitudes and have become as, you might say there, God-ready. I have nothing but praise for all aspects of creation. I have nothing but love for all creatures set adrift to explore the illusions of separation. I have nothing but merry laughter for the cosmic joke the Hindus call maya. And ultimately I have nothing, I am nothing, and I require nothing. It's a wonderful place to be and I invite you all to join me and the many 'me's' surrounding, but only when you're ready."

(13), the priest figure from Akhenaten's days in Ancient Egypt, would also like to speak:

My passion in the old days, to directly connect the incarnate personality to the one God through the realisation of the soul, as opposed to the intercession of a dogma-and-ritual obsessed priesthood, was left stymied by political realities of the day, and although I did not spend too much of my post-mortem Paradise life brooding over lost battles, a good deal of 'my' frustrated desires manifested in the Druid and Christian lives thereafter, finding various measures of what might be termed 'mildly successful' expression but mostly experiencing the great dark repression of those centuries before the Renaissance and Reformation, with their measures of light and learning, where true spiritual impulse was quickly and severely stamped out root and branch. Humans were not ready for an imminent, transcendent God. Their deep-seated fears of a sinful nature and a vengeful deity coupled with a frantic distrust of the predatory Other, circling the family and village, created the repressive religious strictures, demanding aristocracies and inflexible serfdom of their days. The 'later' incarnations of 'my' frustrated impulse watched sadly as ignorance and superstitious fears poisoned the decades as widely as any blight or plague.

Patiently developing a tiny light in an enormous, overpowering dark was their lesson, and the 'me' of those centuries often hovered about their suffering selves, offering as much empathy and understanding as my developing angelic nature would allow. We all of 'us' feel that, given this background, the most successful expression of individual self-determination was, (12), our lady from Venice, who, with two of her related expressions, developed the sensual mothering intelligence, which had been glimpsed, but not fully appreciated, by (14) and (15) in their days, and coupling it with the bemused disregard for the pretensions of authority, both spiritual and temporal, fashioned the template for the oh-so-modern iconoclastic spirituality which so informs Gordon's current expression. We are all very interested to see how Gordon implements the various strands of life energy he has inherited from our expressions in time. Most of us have been 'here', resting in the apparent non-action of the Higher Self for long enough to develop a sophisticated understanding of how the frustration of soul probes and their objectives rise above any sense of temporary defeat and contributes to the subtle diversity of the whole.

The creation of a miniature universe employs all the frustrations of desire and ambition as well as their seeming fulfillment, for the encyclopedia of incarnate experience. Every last smidgen of suffering, joy, laughter, sadness, cunning, bravery, anxiety, you name it, is useful in our endeavour.

"Gordon's enterprise, given the relative freedoms of his era and society, is a marvel of self-expression to most of us. While taking responsibility for his thoughts and actions, and accepting the various karmas thus incurred, Gordon's ability to openly activate so many of the ideas and projects we nurtured in either guilt or secrecy, or both, strikes us as the greatest adventure yet attempted by our group on the planet. That he can openly access the loving and wise embrace of Higher Self, freely write and publish his thoughts and opinions, reach out to many personalities of various persuasions and belief systems, and communicate the Christ light to them as best he can without fear of persecution or retribution, whilst living, what would appear to be, the most mundane and humble of physical plane lives is, to us, as we imbibe the various qualities and textures of the experience to us, along with what he calls, in deference to esoteric tradition, the antahkarana, an amazing liberation of potential. Regardless of the measure of 'success' he achieves, his trailblazing, as well as building upon 'earlier' efforts by us retirees, does, of course, help pave the way for 'future' explorations, of which the soul he calls Cassiopeia, encountered in the second book of this series, is but one.

"In my epoch, during the long reign of Egyptian cultural dominance, many of the psychic abilities and esoteric teachings he takes almost for granted were either birthed or rebirthed and very carefully nurtured. Almost too carefully it would now seem. Some of that care was due to the knowing that our inheritance from Atlantis was freighted with the spectre of misuse and degeneration; we felt that the practice should, as much as possible, be kept free from malign influence from the lower spheres. Purity of motive and precision of discipline were paramount. Our selection and training process was rigorous and perhaps merciless. Deviation from what we felt was a proven formula was barred under any circumstances. We allowed our determination to turn into a moral rigidity and heartless inflexibility. Aspirants died in our care and we consigned them to the 'not-good-enough' heap. But it was excused as a cultural norm, as brutalities of various kinds often are in autocratic regimes. Empires, whether of the sword or the spirit, are forged with steely determination. They cannot be maintained in that fashion, but few Empires ever ascend to that realisation. The pioneers who bravely strive are inevitably followed by bureaucrats who consolidate all gains, including their own, into laws, structures and traditions which strangle the free expression of the life spirit, calling on their own demise from the wings. Egypt made as much of a success of it as any, but I and my two related expressions in that civilisation all saw the coming decline and collapse as inevitable, despite the repeated efforts at regeneration. I knew we contained the seeds of our own demise, and it was despite this that I forged ahead with the one-God project, seeing in it the potential for direct communication, devoid of dogmatic, bureaucratic interference, between individual and deity."

"Gordon has stated that when he enters a deep meditation and moves freely through the time medium, there are only a few 'selves' which seem to recognise the actuality of his efforts, most sensing an angelic visitation of some kind. Well, the other half of that equation is myself, (13), and, (4), both perceived his 'arrival' more or less clearly as a visit from the planet's future and we both derived great inspiration and consolation from the experience. Knowing that the spiritual impulse of our epochs was in decline, it thrilled each of us to feel that all was not lost, that the light of spirit would return, unencumbered, in some more enlightened age. So, in a way, those of us who needed to see Gordon as he was, rather than some nebulous representation of angelic benevolence, were able to, and thus, according to the ancient, unwavering principle, each received according to his need.

Another soul steps forward:

"I am number (10) in the list, and although I chafe at being so anonymously categorised, I understand why this has been selected as the method. We want the reader to see how unimportant our earthbound personalities have become, now that we have finished with their trials. I, perhaps, am still a touch more sensitive about the terms of my treatment, but it remains a trifle. The task is completed and the pain transmuted. Orphaned early, I was chained to a cruel family who made me slave to their whims. Made pregnant by either the son or the father, I know not which, I was mercilessly blamed and made an outcast in a time of widespread intolerance and cruel poverty. I wandered the county, looking for employment whilst trying to hide my true state. Taken in, after many deprivations, by a kindly widow who desperately needed help, I managed to keep my little burden a secret for many months. The widow guessed, I now know, but kept quiet, partly from a natural commiseration and partly from an honest knowing of her own needs. A sudden and unexpected delivery, for which we were quite unprepared, ended with a dead child and a barely breathing mother. Agony mixed with guilty relief was the colour of our days thereafter. Many things we did not speak of as we tended the animals and worked the land. Only the secrets of the eyes were shared. The guilt of course, was knawing away at my insides, as a small animal trapped would try desperately to claw its way out. I was a haunted woman, haunted by my own sin, and fated, I thought, to drag it around with me until death claimed me for his own."

"The widow died suddenly as we were working one day in the field. We had not been natural friends, but she had shown me such kindness I could do nothing but fall on knees beside her and weep. That few minutes between us, although she was growing colder by the moment, were the most intimate between us, the most intimate I'd shared with anyone in that short and sad life."

"I did what I thought was right and necessary. A burial in the village graveyard, a letter to distant relatives. A man came with another letter. He was authorised to sell the property and I was to leave. I had a month in which the sale of animals was to be arranged. I left before the new owners arrived, not wishing to lend them the pleasure of eviction. I took what little money I had amassed, my few clothes, and boarded the morning coach. Taking a tiny room above a tavern in the big city, I slept and crept about my days, seeking out funds as best I could. Lonely, sad, and burdened with worthlessness and self-loathing, I spent my last few weeks providing the ale drinkers with the quick comfort they sought and the few pence I needed. I soon became the victim I craved. The end was quick and brutal, a blade to the guts and a laughing urination on my corpse. A heap of waste in the gutter, not even a groan in the dark and rain."

"The tales of wandering souls were true; I quickly became one myself, roaming the fields and lanes and woods of my county, taking some small pleasure in the waning autumn months, yet sure the devil was to take my soul, and was merely toying with me, as a cat plays with the mouse he has cornered. In death I felt closer to the fields, trees, rivers, and even the tiny wildflowers, than I ever had when alive. They'd always been my friends, but now they seemed to be reaching out to me as I used to reach out to them. Lying in the fields for what seemed a small forever I felt their little musical whisperings wash over me, a benediction rarely given in my short sad life."

"Sometimes I felt as though I would have been happier and maybe even more useful as a part of the land. I would sit by trees and ask them how I could become one of them. Some would not reply; others would tell me I could not do such a thing, that I was human and had to remain so. It was not an answer I wanted to hear, but it was given in such a caring spirit that it did not seem to matter. I made myself content just to wander the land like some nearly happy ghost, like a tree who magically sprouted legs. The many animals of the fields and forests seemed to know my presence, some keeping their distance and others coming close to inspect and maybe become a friend. I had always had a vague notion, when alive and miserable, that I would be better as a hermit in the woods, but never had the courage to strike out in that way. In my wanderings I happened upon one such creature, someone old and stooped with a stern visage that refused to recognise me as I sat outside her shack on a rock and watched. She busied herself with many activities, the collecting and drying of herbs being one I was sure of. I stayed for days, absorbing myself in her mysterious routines. On the third night as she slept and I lay resting, never now feeling the need for sleep and not knowing why, but for the deep conviction that the dark one had me in his grip, she came to me, hovering like an angel, a light all around her. She knew who I was and what ailed me, how, I do not know, but the affections I felt overwhelmed me and I sobbed like a child."

"I was a chained spirit who should be free from Earth and its sufferings. I should be in Heaven with all the happy children. I knew I was wicked and destined for the other place and I told her so. She said 'wait for me here' and was gone. In moments she returned with a shining one who looked like the blessed mother herself. I couldn't believe she would come to save a fallen woman like me but she stood there smiling and welcoming. I melted into her arms and was, I don't know, somewhere else right away. A beautiful place, a garden, maybe that first garden where Eve made her big mistake."

"It wasn't of course, but it was heaven, and my guide was not who I thought but a caring member of my group soul, the lady of wealth and influence from Venice, (12), who would now like to take up the reigns of the tale, our tale."

(12): Venetian courtesan:

"My own journey though the Renaissance era in Venice was one of resolute determination on all fronts. It seemed like a lifelong battle against the status quo at the time, but now I know I was working on what you call in your day 'the divine feminine', and that the lives of other women in the group were feeding my strategies. Much can you discover if you survive the drama of your incarnation and still wish to learn the deep roots of your struggles. Paradise can be an education too.

"I was told by a wise friend that my strength could help others, others not so fortunate, so I willingly accompanied her and found myself peering onto Earth again, looking down as I used to think angels did. I was shown the sad days of (11) and saw, without instruction, how I could help. I tried to inspire her at almost every difficult turn in her short life, but her lack of self-worth and her self-loathing proved too high a hurdle. Yet, in the place of the irritation and frustration, which I might have felt at her shortcomings had I known her on Earth, I felt a growing tenderness, as if she were my own orphan, my own inward child ('inner' as you say now), cowering behind the bold front I fabricated for society, and when she passed on from her ignoble death, and I was restrained from trying to take vengeance upon her attackers, I was eventually persuaded that saving her from herself was the most fruitful plan of attack. And so I appeared, after much patient observation, as the angelic entity accompanying the kind witch and, as you can see, was able to use the poor soul's projection of her deepest spiritual need as the transport to another dimension, a world where she could be reunited not only with her lost child but also her soul family.

"I did not know it, but I was in training then, not to be my idea of an angel, but to be as many souls' idea of an angel as possible. That, as you may imagine, involves discovering in one's heart the merciful, forgiving love of God, and holding it there, as if it were the one driving force behind your being, so that when a troubled soul looks to you for guidance, their image of merciful love is what they see."

"Never having believed the hurled condemnations of the ecclesiastics of my day, I had already dwelt in the Paradise of my dreams and enjoyed it wholeheartedly and was ready for some new challenge. Those who are watching, and they always are, whether you are aware of it or not, take note, and bring you a proposal which befits your state. I was then ready for the type of challenge offered and I soon found myself working with (11), as I have indicated. After removing her from the fields of pain in which she wandered, seeking solace and companionship from the spirits of nature and seeing that she was placed in the home of rest and recuperation most fitting to her state, I was shown how others might be helped."

"The passing from the Paradise world to the Earth seemed so simple that I wondered why I had not thought to so journey myself. My guides brought me to several scenes of women in distress, some in the throes of bloody birth, some abandoned to barrenness, some waiting for a husband's return, and some who struggled in poverty, their man gone. We moved back and forth from scene to scene that I might become fully acquainted with, not only the human actors, but also the passage between them. For not only did they exist in different societies, but their eras were separated by hundreds of years. I was to be travelling through time as well as space. I rested in my Paradise home to contemplate these shocks. As I had earlier achieved a goodly measure of earthly wealth, I had felt drawn to a humble abode, a sweet nest in the hills, where the soul could rest undisturbed in bowers of birdsong and leaf rustle. Some of my old colleagues had opted for the grand and opulent in their choice of Paradise house, and dwelt in small cities with impressive architecture and fountains galore. Their comfort was in the spectacular, mine in the chaste green seclusions of Mother

Nature. On visiting, they looked at me fondly and spoke indulgently of my retirement."

"Of my new role in the Paradise world I did not speak, for I hardly knew what to say. Instead I talked of the nature of poetry that I composed in moments of idleness; this they understood. Such is the happiness of the Paradise world, where none may oppress with demanding laws or dogma, that one dares not disturb the joys of the formerly imprisoned with thoughts that may disturb. My wise friend visited and asked if I was reconciled to my new status. I said I did not care for this status but I did wish for useful employment. This seemed to be the reply she sought and we smiled together, silent conspirators in Godly mercy.

"So began my career of roving inspirer, the human agent of divine embrace. My own children in my Earth life were my model, as indeed a mother's true love is the human copy of the sacred one. Of course, my understanding of God's love was severely tried by the judgments and hypocrisy of his self-appointed agents on Earth. As I struggled with their deceitful ways and fought to keep my faith untainted, I was aided in a secret way by others in the group, whose faith in the face of earthly problems remained strong and pure, mainly (1), (4), and (18). No secret now of course, to me or to you, but back then I knew nothing of soul groups and inter-dimensional energetic links.

I believe you can well imagine my inspired career, from scene to scene I moved, charging my poor creatures with the energy of courage and determination in their situations of turmoil and incipient defeat. (7), (9), (11), (19) and (20) were all unconscious recipients of my subtle ministrations. Their angers, frustrations, and black despairs were my challenges. I would arrive at (7)'s life, a middle class wife and mother in a market town of what you call Ancient China as she would be nervously anticipating the arrival home of her demanding and short-tempered husband. I would aim the energy of courage into her heart, hoping that it would overcome her innate sense of low worth. This would often make her slow her fussing and look pensive for a few moments and some hints of the resolute would flicker and settle. Then I would appear in another country and time, much in the future from when I was on Earth. There, in what you would call Victorian era Britain, (9), would be playing with her dolls and toys with her mother close by, attending to the cook and various household functions. The contentment and pleasure in this child's life was a joy to behold. When her mother appeared from time to time, their love bond filled the room with its light. Having been advised that this was a happy home, I did little but observe, and wonder what my function might be. The father was a country doctor, after the fashion of the day, and was often gone. And although he and the mother had their difficulties, a truce had been achieved and the home did not significantly darken when he appeared from time to time."

"From there I would move to (11), who, awaiting her husband's return from a long voyage, would often wait by the shore near the harbour, looking out to sea and praying when her child slept. It had been months with no reports or even rumours. The money that had been left was slowly disappearing. An insidious panic gripped her heart. I attempted to weaken its deadly embrace with the energy of optimism, of happier futures. She felt these efforts as dreams, as the desperation of one who is hopelessly condemned. She knew she was clutching at straws. I wanted to know where her husband was, lost, stranded, living in another country with another wife, but I knew not how to go about this search, did not even know such a project was possible for one like me.

"Later I would discover, but then I merely hoped for the best as I moved swiftly to (19), a daughter of noble birth left pregnant in her father-in-law's castle while her husband was called to war. On Earth I had raised children on my own, as courtesans rarely married. My status and wealth ensured fine apartments and servants, so it was not so much a struggle but more a daily challenge of household management, something I found much to my liking. But my confidence and organising skills made little impression on (19), who floundered in a sea of conflicting emotions, barely acknowledging the child growing in her womb, desperate for the safe return of her betrothed, fretting about her looks and worrying about the over-zealous attentions of her husband's father, taking solace only in the devotions of her lady-in-waiting. I sensed I was to bide my time with her and concentrate for the moment on her twin soul, (20), a young widow in late 19th century Canada, a country unknown in my time. She was also awaiting a husband at sea, pacing her rooms and her town in an ever-increasing desperation. I could make no headway with her and turned to my wise friend for help."

"Having assumed her wisdom would be the solution I was surprised to hear that Gordon was to be called on, as his twentieth century talents were ripe for such a challenge. Although I would soon become familiar with his soul energy and activities in the planes, Gordon was a complete stranger to me at this juncture. When I was filled in on the progress of his abilities, I felt he would have been called a magus in my time. My wise guide explained that in his era, both religions and governments had lost so much of their grip upon the citizen that individuals were more or less free to pursue both their talents and inclinations without harassment. In his time people like him were known as meditators and practitioners of consciousness projection, whatever that was."

"My friend explained that he could move his being about through space and time while still living on Earth, and as he served the light he could assist souls in distress. I was shown his method. It involved lying down on his bed, placing soft black cups with strings stretching from them over his ears, and closing his eyes as if to rest. After some time he emerged out of his own body, looking more or less like his true self and floated away through the walls of his chambers. He mainly attended to souls lost between the worlds, those sad, confused specters who scare both peasant and aristocrat with their rumblings and moanings. The soft black cups over his ears were little machines which conveyed sounds to his ears that, while mingling in his brain, allowed his soul to shake free of its fleshy encasement and fly wherever spirit called for assistance. His method was to approach a lost soul as a friend, engaging them in what looked to me like idle chatter and jokes, only slowly bringing about the subject of the heavens and their inhabitants. In my own time on Earth I had learned, and indeed excelled, at the art of making others relaxed and comfortable. It became that I could charm the sour temper of almost any friend or stranger, man or woman, and they were more than happy to reward me generously for such a service. As Gordon seemed willing to do the same for little or no reward, I was prepared to offer him saintly status, but my wise friend surprised me by saying that his abilities were a direct result of mine and that I should be proud of my contribution. Gordon, she said, was benefiting from the experience of many beings, and that he was like unto a great chef who could combine, at will, the many ingredients which would result in a dish of marvellous subtleties."

"His latest advance was to do his consciousness projection in public places without the benefit of the soft black cups and their strange magic. We watched as he sat on a bench in the lovely garden of an old church and projected a part of himself out of his body, and then, without actually moving, passed backwards through time, to the home of the troubled soul with whom I had no luck. He found her in a drunken rampage. Wailing, she flung herself from wall to wall of her bedroom, in an orgy of destructive intoxication. My guide wanted me to see how Gordon was discovering abilities in himself he had not known existed.

One was the ability to make a brief appearance on Earth and make his influence felt. He understood that he could influence the ghostly lost souls of his regular practice, but to be a temporary ghost and influence the living, that he did not know of. My guide explained talents like that go from life to life, but the personality does not always know of their presence. I asked her what she meant by 'go from life to life'. Did she mean the transmigration of souls, as I had heard whispered in many late night conversations, most often by those who had journeyed to the East or were intimate with those who had? Yes, was her answer.

"So after we had watched Gordon, through commanding presence and calm but firm instruction, gain the attentions of our frantic lady, she took me off to instruct me in more detail about the movement of souls from life to life. Before we departed, however, I was fascinated to see the lady fall at Gordon's feet in the painful supplication of weeping and realise she took him for an angel, although to us he appeared just like Gordon lying in his twentieth century bedroom with the soft black cups about his ears.

"My instruction on transmigration, although a great revelation, did not shock me as it might have on Earth. Somehow it seemed right, almost as if I had secretly known this truth, but like so many other truths in my hypocritical society, had to be publicly denied so that a tranquil life might be maintained. When my guide mentioned the Indian man sitting crossed legged with his eyes firmly shut that I often used to dream about and wonder why, I gasped, for she was right. The Indian man with the shaved head was my lifelong puzzle and secret. Was he who I was? Yes, she said firmly, but he was only one of who I was, yet perhaps more intimately connected than the others. This, of course, intrigued me, but my guide felt I had been given 'enough to chew on for now' and left me to continue my rounds, as she called it. This being, as you know, is (26), and will speak anon.

"Sometime later I witnessed Gordon continue his angel act and further invest the distressed lady with the salve of love. He appealed to her deeper religious nature and suggested she continue her life in a way her saviour would approve of. Later he brought her spirit husband to her, giving him the power to manifest for a few precious seconds. The lady was so happy and grateful I longed to be able to perform such a graceful function myself. I would, of course learn, finally becoming so adept at the soul transformations and projections that I could easily qualify, in your modern terms, as an aspect of the divine feminine, although wearing the mantle of such grand conceptions is a role I would readily retire from, were it not for the needs of those I work with. I feel more like an actor in this eternity of action, one who constantly changes costumes, depending on which vision my audience that day requires. I now travel through time as easily as you move from kitchen to bedroom, inspiring those in the forgetful flesh as each situation requires, and retire to my home in the spirit worlds when the storms of fear and desire have momentarily subsided.

(26): A Buddhist monk speaks:

"I am (26) and do not wish to burden you with many words and concepts, for they are all, however grand or profound, illusions of the self-regarding intellect, and need to be discarded, along with all the demons, ideologies, and deities which have blighted your path with their temporary allures. You belong, as I do, in the Buddha fields, the pure land of perfection, where life is calm emptiness, drained of the tempests of anxious activity, and nothing remains to be done or even contemplated. Here, in the radiant void, beyond the ravishing excitements of bliss, we, who are no longer differentiated, are settled into the stillness of not only non-action but also non-being, and know not happiness nor unhappiness, desire or lack of desire. The glamorous trap of existence no longer tempts us.

"I touched this non-place in my monk's meditations many times in that land of time and saw that this was the destiny of the sham some call soul. Many of my fellows knew only the teachings, the learning by rote, the prescribed rituals, and what ought to eventually happen, but I penetrated through prayer and ritual to the promised land beyond nirvana. In my brief sojourns there, I understood what had been taught and more. The vanity of all human ambition was laid bare, not only by death, but in the ultimate illusion of manifestation: all that exists, all sentience compelled into form, is sustained by the needs and fears of other forms. *One is there because the other is there*; neither *can* exist without the other, and neither *does* exist without the other. What would we do without existence? They squeal to each other silently behind their courting smiles. Where is the meaning of our trials, the significance of our inscrutable deities, where is the meaning of our search for meaning? In the shining of the radiant void, all this vanity is absorbed and digested. Nothing can flourish and blossom into endless multiplicity, but the endless clever creativity all returns to its source, begetting nothing."

"The requirements of the bodhisattva, and the allure which comes with them, did not tempt me. All is vanity: all prophets, teachers, angels, deities. Pride, ambition, compassion, mercy; all are equally foolish, endeavours composed of emptiness. Without them, of course, we would not have manifested life. They, of course, argue for their own usefulness. Souls are lost in the wilderness and cry out for their ministrations; compassion compels a response. They sacrifice their nirvana for the needs of others they brag, wearing their renunciation like a badge of honour in a field of reprobates. But what they don't tell you is that their service is not actually needed; that is, any more than any other manifestation is needed, or that their prolonged fit of do-gooderism is balancing out their earlier adventures in the realms of selfish accumulations of glamour and power. All the good guys were bad guys once: heroes and villains in the children's book of life. None of it matters ultimately; no planet, no culture, no religion, no God. Transcending the mess, draining every last drip of desire, and reuniting with the radiant void above and beyond the call of God and his stuff; that and only that should be your goal. It was and is *mine*, as much as *mine* is merely a temporary transport to the place of no-place."

Higher Self/Monad:

"The above are some of my honoured guests and family members, and I thank them all for sharing their stories. Each one has contributed immeasurably to my understanding of life on planet Earth. Without them and those like them I would still be a Monad, an indivisible unit of the divine, but I would be an empty one, an ocean of potential without any waves of activity. Now I am almost ready to help supervise the start-up and running of a new planetary being, if such a graduation should be my chosen mode of expression. It could be the new Earth being readied for those who are/will be unable to make that evolutionary leap which has been termed the ascension process, or perhaps another experiment of which I am as yet unaware. In such a situation I, and other Monads, will be as shepherds rather than administrators, overseeing the development of sentience in a myriad of forms yet to be devised. Doubtless some of us will become revered as deities, and awarded attributes we have no desire to own, and others will be seen as angelic messengers, bringing divine instruction to a needy populace. These roles, although thrust upon us – as incarnate beings project their desires upon our light – will be something we have to either adapt to or make allowance for. We will be immensely intelligent beings of light who will be called upon time and time again to manifest qualities and personas relevant to the emotional, mental and spiritual needs of the individuals and societies under our tutelage."

"Our ability to access these roles has been completely facilitated by the almost inestimable contribution of our many soul probes, as the data accumulated from their incarnate adventures provides us with an encyclopedia of experiential reference points. So again, let me emphasise that *we* are *you* as much as *you* are *us*. The Monad and the Soul are one. All that remains, all that ever remains, is for the incarnate personality to understand and embrace this."

"Many, certainly, have a long and difficult journey in this accomplishment. Some are trapped in the willful imprisonment and self-flagellation of the hell realms, others in the pleasure soaked flattery of the various Paradises, and yet others in the devotional pieties of their religion's appointed heaven. All these beings separate themselves from the God consciousness in their desire to remain just who they are – either a depraved version or a radiant one – but whether soiled in sin or resurrected in purity they are still *separated*. Until they renounce identity and disappear into the nothingness of *the all*, they do not know and they cannot share."

12

GORDON'S TAKE ON IT, SO FAR

As Gordon has begun the process of fully embracing the understanding that the *Monad and the Soul are one*, it seems appropriate to allow him the opportunity to express his experience of the Monad/Soul relationship. He knows he is only part way along this journey, but sees that a progress report, however partial, would be of great use at this point in the unfolding.

Gordon: "Glancing at the list of characters I see I am at the head. This careless ascription, penned in haste by yours truly, implies a ranking of significance, but let me quickly add that is not how I see it, or myself. Of course, I am no more important than any other soul in the unfolding, I am merely the latest in linear time."

"That souls belong to groups called Monads, although a major and perhaps shocking discovery on the journey of spiritual awakening, 'Gordon' often wonders about its, shall we say, experiential relevance. We're all souls, we're all evolving at one rate or another, and we all belong to one Monad or another. Beyond making the playing field about as even as you could want, it does not seem to affect actual experience or potential outcome in any significant way. I do 'feel' closer to some of those in 'my' Monad than others, probably because we share characteristics and aspirations, but my level of love for them seems not to outstrip my appreciation of incarnate souls encountered in my day to day existence, either on the planet or in the spheres whilst out of body."

"Of course, given the unconditional nature of the love energy we are developing, that should not be surprising, but I wonder, as I continue to open myself to more and wider vistas of sentience, what qualities, if any, are specific to my 'soul family' relationships. Intimacy? A sharing of a common goal? Yes, but these do not seem to obstruct or interfere with one's wide range of activities. They are just one more activity. Certainly, as one moves away from the genetic imperatives, blood lust and folk-soul directives of family, tribe, and nation, one is reluctant to reinsert one's freed self into yet another club with its conditions and fearful concerns. The only fraternity one wishes to recognise is that of all sentient beings."

"Gordon feels the presence/influence of the other souls in his group almost constantly, and has done for years. Initially, due to the partial unveiling of the past-life regression process, he felt only two or three, and worked at accommodating the shock of their arrival. That one was a philosopher of some renown was not any help; he knew revealing the relationship would cast him as foolish and deluded. That another had been a king seemed not to help matters either, and he kept that one deeply under wraps. Later, after years of massaging his resistance, through the modalities of dream, vision, and sudden insight, the small group was slowly increased, and eventually he could trace their various influences in his abilities, character traits, and the various affiliations and attributes of the emotional and mental bodies. The more he placed his motivations and choices under close examination, the more he seemed to see that his character was an ingenious blend of many others, as if elements had been refined and recombined for a new, improved version. And there were occasions when he wondered if Gordon was unique only in as much as a new recipe was being tried out by a star chef whose reputation was for inspired improvising."

"There were certain experiences which seemed to shout 'Here's a new confluence of influences'. One was his sudden immersion in hands-on healing, which he suddenly decided should be the next stage on his path. Without pre-meditation he felt he knew exactly what was needed in the situation, how to channel the energy, how to invoke the source, how to deal with the ancient scars on the etheric and astral bodies and the various entities stuck within his clients. Probing further he sensed the loving ministrations of mothers, the blessings of priests, the sexual mothering of courtesans, the energy work practiced in Atlantis and

Egypt, and the innate knowledge of the mystic applied to specifics. The influences of (5), (13), (14), (18), and (22) could all be clearly felt. In his writing (2), (3), (13), (15) and (16) were very much present. In his emotional relationships with either sex, a large selection of the cast was perceived as influential. For example, when in retreat from sexual situations, the energy of (3), (11), (12), (17), and (25) could all be felt. When thus engaged, it was (6), (9), (13), (15), (18), (21) and (23)."

"You have likely guessed that there were few, if any, life situations, where the soul influence of one or several of the others could not be felt. Predictably Gordon would wonder just where 'he' ended and the others took over. Imagined boundaries, when more carefully examined, would quickly dissipate. If he was feeling, say, timid, in a particular situation with certain pressures, he could feel where the timidity of some of the others were feeding his, and then, later, feel that the energy of timidity had them all in its grip, and that his efforts in overcoming could actually help them all. Extending this to the entire range of emotional and mental complexes he began to see that all his 'soul family', as he came to think of them, were swimming, as it were, in seas of emotional and mental energy, and that their difficulties and challenges were specific versions, or perhaps local variations, of universal encounters. He could also see this as analogous to the genetically defined family unit, which gathered karma, traits, desire, and conflicts into another fluid grouping of challenges to the psyche. Certainly there was more than one way to define a family."

"Although we are merged, let me use an image here: I hold 'Gordon' at arm's length, watching his behaviour as he moves through his days. This is what many traditions encourage disciples to develop: the observer consciousness, as it aids immeasurably in understanding the rather robotic consciousness of the personality, with its panoply of fears and unconscious drives. Practised sufficiently, sometimes months, sometimes years, it can lead to a significantly more harmonious relationship between the personality and the soul. 'Gordon' found he could not avoid it, no matter how hard he tried. As much as thirty-five years before these words are composed, he felt this observing eye through most of his waking hours and, realising it was more than mere shame-tinged self-consciousness, wondered why these various traditions felt it was necessary to work toward this state. Some years passed before he saw that he must have developed this in other lives, and the emergence of the past-life regression literature, with its emphasis on past-life efforts manifesting as natural abilities in the current incarnation, only confirmed the insight. So now, when I hold 'Gordon' at arm's length and observe, he knows what exactly is going on. He knows he is an actor whose performance is always being rated and recorded. But he tells me he no longer cares and is happy to improvise every move in the ongoing game of his life. I am welcome to his emotions, thoughts, and spiritual strivings, mainly because he feels no distance between us. He says 'Gordon' has been merged with his soul. Maybe 'subsumed' would be more accurate. He certainly feels contained in me, his soul. And, perhaps needless to say, we both, as one, feel a direct line of awareness to Monad."

"Although I often feel like a mixture of many people, all of whom are having a say in how I act, react, think, and feel, I know that I am yet unique, an individual and unrepeatable blend of character traits designed to accomplish a variety of incarnational tasks and projects, so that the way is cleared of as much karmic debris as possible, and the post-ascension plateau can be freely used for the next stage of challenges. Of course, that phrase 'post-ascension' tickles one's fancy. What will the post-ascension phase actually be like? One can imagine and embellish but one cannot say for certain, as the outcomes depend largely on the efforts and accomplishments of every soul actively involved. Perhaps an outline is all one can produce with any degree of credibility."

"I, as I'm currently constituted, imagine that many of the abilities of the present vanguard of psychic explorers will be well within the reach of the bulk of the populace, although likely the adventurous/reckless young will be the true inheritors of the clairvoyant, clairsentient, and telepathic spectrum emerging. Astral consciousness will be well within the grasp of many. Meditators, some aided by the brain modulating functions of subliminal sound waves, will readily envision the goings on in various astral planes and, I suspect, even daydreamers, say on the verge of an afternoon nap, will find themselves slipping in and out of the astral. Of course many will mistake it for a conventional dream, but sightings and hearings of deceased loved ones will offset this. Nature lovers of all kinds will feel an unusual closeness to the spirits behind the forms they so love and many will sight the fairies and devas they have only read about previously. Even those who use their ecological concerns to cajole others into frenzies of shame will find their inspiration undercut with a deeper vision of adaptability of ensouled nature."

"And of course, if one or other of the inventors currently working on trans-dimensional 'telephones' manages to bring their vision into working manifestation, the resulting constant communication between the 'living' and the 'dead' will transform 'life' in ways almost impossible to imagine from our current position, although I strongly suspect it will not, in itself, bring about Heaven on Earth. That we will still have to strive for, as tribal and religious loyalties and internecine warfare will still have their desperate adherents. As you may know, several teams are currently working on such technical developments and, although it will be easy, with 20/20 hindsight, to say it was manifested exactly when we were ready for it, there are too many variables to prophesy its arrival from the 'now' of this writing. There are, and will be, those who would decry its development as 'demonic' in nature and will do their best to deny and suppress its use. Whether their innate negativity is currently affecting the flowering of its development is a matter of some discussion amongst those involved. It is not for me to dispose of the matter with magisterial pronouncements, but I cannot fail to observe that the interaction of human emotions and thoughts with their environment, is as yet an unrecognised science."

"Ask yourself this: are we, as a society, ready to give up our fear of death, our hope for Heaven, our anger at God, our relentless self-judgement, and all the psychic impediments we put in the way of fully confronting these issues? Are we? Regular and easy contact with our 'dead' will deeply impact on all these matters. Much anxiety will be gladly swept away in the initial euphoria, but much goal oriented activity will soon seem somehow empty, leading many to a painful and slow reassessment of life activities. The young, as always, will lead the way in embracing the sudden and exciting realities, but I suspect an entire generation will evaporate from the physical before the shock of the new becomes the calm of the norm. And of course, many will shun the developments as new-fangled, weird, and just generally undesirable, not to mention the millions whose religious leaders will forcibly condemn the developments as issuing from the dark side of deceit. Since it is written that the dead shall not rise till judgement day, how can they possibly speak, unless they are demons bent on our enslavement?"

"And if, as many suspect, the 'dead' begin to interact with us through the internet, the phenomenon will spread like wildfire, as they say, although the sceptics will multiply almost as rapidly, for the appearance of the miraculous always seems to be accompanied by legions of naysayers champing at the bit to expose the popular delusion."

"For a current example, look no further than the crop circle phenomenon. After decades of staggeringly complex and aesthetically breathtaking formations, it cannot be said that humanity has altered course in any significant way because of it. If faith and inspiration has been renewed for some, a passionate fringe fomenting inner revolution, for many it is a cause for caustic merriment, one more example of the credulous buying into yet another scam, and for others it is barely worth a passing mention. Other 'miraculous' sightings, such as those of the Blessed Virgin Mary, evoke a similar range of response, suggesting that humanity's need for the miraculous is balanced by its urge to remain boxed in the predictable mundane."

"One of the most powerful religions on the planet is sceptical materialism; its high priests are the all-powerful scientists who are called upon to pronounce on every development, and its enforcers the cynical, *common sense* journalists who dictate our opinions daily. Its hold is all the more powerful for not being recognised. If the iron grip of three dimensions is the dream from which we are all trying to awaken, and history is its accompanying nightmare, then the *common sense* prescription of the sceptical materialist supervisors is the potion which keeps us entranced by our own limitations. We cannot expand because we fervently wish to stay boxed in. How much this state of affairs will continue in the face of all the aspects of the ascension process remains to be seen, but I suspect it will continue to play a defining role."

"Will thinking positively aid in the launch of this new reality? Absolutely. But in entertaining those positive thought projections, let us remember that our doubts and fears bubble away under the surface and help create much more conservative (read tame) consensus realities. Of course, the creation and maintenance of consensus realities is a subject which requires an entire book of its own, but suffice to say that we all contribute in some small way, even if it's only acquiescence. The meshing of our collective desire to be accepted and our perceived limitation of the possible is so complete and pervasive that we cannot, except in moments of heightened awareness, actually see it. For reasons more to do with conformity and contentment we have imprisoned ourselves in the daily grind of our own design. To step outside this consensus reality is to see craziness enacting its own validation with hive mentality making sure its members contribute to the reassuring conformity. To stay outside for too long is to become anti-social and weird and eventually to court accusations of insanity. Fortunately the days when one could be locked up for exploring the freedoms of the non-conditioned response to moment to moment reality seem to be over. Nowadays we just drug our repeat offenders into docility and allow their eccentricities to flourish on the street."

"Of course the ascension process will take us far beyond setting free the manic and unstable to improvise their existence without external restraints. Hopefully it will set us all free to explore the vast untapped potential of our consciousness while we are still physically alive, so that the magical reality of the between-life state will be more than merely a vague dream or wish-fulfillment fantasy. How much of our astral reality will be able to manifest in our post-ascension physical reality cannot be predicted, as it really depends on our ability to open ourselves beyond the reach of our doubts. Will people be able to manifest their food merely by thinking it into existence? Well it's a daily practice on the astral among those of our dead who still feel the desire for conventionally attractive nourishment, so theoretically it should be possible. Will people fly or teleport? Again, it's a very possible yes, although perhaps not for fifty to a hundred years. As the base vibration of the physical plane increases to closer to that of the astral, many fantasies will become possible, but just how many really depends on our ability to accept the advent of the miraculous. Just as now, when our doubts and fears manifest as fast as our desires, at this not-so-distant future, the same polarity of consciousness will be apparent."

"I suspect there will be a transition period when reports will emerge from the more adventurous that such manifestations have occurred, but they will immediately be doubted, the witnesses suspected of fraud, and film of the events accused of the kind of digital manipulation available even today. There will be those who will fearlessly walk barefoot on the hot coals, those who choose not to, those who will deny the possibility, and those who will scoff at the mere idea and assume wilful deception at the outset. Film of someone flying a few feet can easily be faked they will say. Witnesses can be bought and the credulous will believe anything."

"Look at the disbelief cast at all the UFO footage of recent years. There are those who just refuse to see. They don't like it, don't want it, so let's forget it. The thousands of detailed abduction reports: they bend some people's reality concepts so out of shape they can't stand it and they just turn away. It's delusion, mass delusion, it's demonic, it's deception. It doesn't exist because it can't exist. It's not in our holy book so it's bullshit."

"Denial can dampen the threat of any enthusiasm and will continue to do so in this transition period and beyond. Some commentators see human nature changing radically in a few short years; I do not disagree, but I see many pockets of resistance, many deep pockets and much circling of the wagons to repel a discomfiting new reality. That's not to say it won't be fascinating and exciting for those who choose to participate, but the sudden appearance of those heavenly upper astral conditions seems unlikely. A more gradual unfolding I suspect. Some clairvoyance here, some telepathy there; folk who lose their interest in meals and don't know why; people who dream so lucidly and continuously of their dear departed that the effects of continuous consciousness begin to creep in upon daily lives. People who say they feel more awake when asleep than when actually awake. And who can actually calibrate the full effects of the so-called '100th monkey effect'? Will the children of people who practise out of body travel and consciousness projection find the abilities surface with little or no effort? Will the so-called Indigo Children increase in numbers, making their healing and telepathic talents almost commonplace? There's a lot of maybes there, and I'm not sure it's worth trying to penetrate the clouds of possibilities, as any number of affecting factors can come into play. And that, in a way, is what's mysteriously exciting about this whole evolutionary project. No-one, including, I believe, the ascended masters, knows exactly how it will turn out. Suffice to say we're definitely headed up the narrowing spiral and out into the freedom of the next level of light, but the rate of our ascent is dependent on so many apparently conflicting factors that any computations seem too booby-trapped with unsuspected surprises to make any effort worthwhile. So let us just move forward with the kind of playful curiosity that feels appropriate to the cause."

13

HOW HIGHER SELF SEES THE SAME THING

While it is appropriate and necessary for Gordon to view the possibilities of the so-called ascension process as a passenger on a train would observe the progress of his journey, Monads like 'me' are not limited to such perspectives. We are free to observe the passage of the train through each landscape, whether urban or rural, not forgetting that each soul probe is travelling on a different train to a different destination. We know, of course, that every destination, although unique, provides the same opportunities for growth, the same challenges of adaptation and assimilation of experience, the same benefits of accomplishment through constriction and trial. We observe and absorb all the experiential information which comes our way and, to use your modern metaphor, file it away for 'future' use. And although we are virtually omniscient by human standards we are always aware that our wisdom is dependent on the information gathering abilities of our soul probes, and we prefer to see ourselves as children of the divine out on an afternoon's adventure rather than the demanding and pompous lesser deities designed by primitive man in his terrified search for security.

Every cultural, religious and political advance that is established in man's quest for a better, safer, and more satisfying life is noted by us. And every setback, in any of those fields of endeavour, acclimatises our appreciation of the nature of duality at the physical level. We would not say 'for every step forward there are two steps back' but we understand how frustrated humans come to see the process in that light. We know that almost every human personality is limited by the span of their incarnation and cannot envision the giant scope of the historical enterprise this planetary project entails. Setbacks, if not exactly written into the script, are allowed for. The most renowned example being, of course, the Atlantean collapse. Centuries of work abandoned; catastrophe denied and then finally embraced; the drawing board cleared for the next inscription. Millions of soul probes recovering on the astral. Not unlike, I might add, the millions of soul probes recovering after World War One. And there is the key for our perception of the 'ascension process'. We have seen it before in a variety of guises – often the renewal charged by a new prophet's arrival – although this effort, moving pan-culturally right across the board, as it were, seems to promise much greater returns. So many of the wounded are ready to be healed, and so much karma is ready to be relinquished. Ah, yes, souls do hang on to their karma. Attachment to wounds and resentment fuels many an incarnation. Look at all those souls that cycle endlessly through the astral/physical duality without ever rising above to truly 'return home'. They spent a lot of time and effort acquiring all that baggage; do you think they're going to just let it all go at the first opportunity?

We see a general lightening of the load, a willingness to soar despite the usual fears, a creative blending of the physical and astral illusions so that the terror of dissolution completely loses its grip, freeing up great bundles of energy for other, more exciting challenges. Yes, it will be a graduation of sorts for some, and perhaps many. There will be souls who will never return to the physical or the astral, residing on the higher formless planes or returning to us as multidimensional files in Monad.

Many souls will require the strengthening of the personality which will occur with the exercise of these newly freed-up energies and, although in a deeper sense that will leave them further mired in the illusion of separation, it will be good for them to feel the power and practice its arts. It will give them the taste of godliness they need to balance their centuries of dependency and self-subjection.

writers learn from each other. Unconsciously of course,
ning goes on just the same. Some of them, in meditation
ve felt obscure presences and vague apprehensions that
working alone. Some assume this to be a divine assistance
ard of long devotion; others shun what might be tempta-
monic seduction of pride and vanity. Only (2), (5), (14), and
and the presence of others, who could be a team tackling
oject with the restrictions of their time and place serving
dicap in the eternal game. Only (1) seems to fully under-
each of the combined efforts, although he insists that (5)
not far behind. (1) sees himself as the consummate team
fiting from all the earlier creative efforts and building on
ng more or less lost his ego based personality value system
er consciousness of the soul and Higher Self, he sees the
y of this 'loss through merging'. While the gratification in-
ompleting the project is palpable and pleasurable, like an
ing an award, he would wish to thank everyone who has
to the achievement so far. He knows full well how much
from the current epoch, where individual freedom is at an
h and societal limitations at an all time low.
is level of personal freedom allows him the mental and psy-
o envision greater and greater portions of his now seemingly
urce? And surely Cassiopeia will uncover even more? Yes to
ow utters questions I've heard before. Like, where does my
ve off and the Godhead 'begin'? How many aspects of 'Gor-
the worlds of spirit, actively engaged in constructive activi-
en were they brought into being? Before 'he' was physically
s other 'team members' were slipped into incarnation? And
vered them before. But he has not allowed himself to hear.
e it's the last tenacious gripping onto his old outmoded be-
that's doing it. Why he's clinging to this more than some-
he is not sure, but clinging he certainly is.
misdemeanors of (22) and his associates of the Atlantean
t? He's been resisting that, he knows. Would acknowledging
tuality of his energy work in that era force him to confront
ration of astral counterparts 'now'? I smirk and nod and he
guesses that's a yes.
stepped forward from his 'file cabinet in my databanks' to
count of his adventures way back when. And adventure is
ncept to be conveyed: 'In Atlantean times we played with

We see souls becoming lighter and freer, less encumbered by the limitations of ancient belief systems, and more enraptured by the possibilities of expansion. We see joy and rapture, and, of course, the fresh challenges implicit in the new vibratory pattern. The new plateau of experience will provide great vistas of fresh inspiration and those who gladly take up the challenge will find rewards and difficulties in equal measure. Duality, despite the wishes of many, will not deteriorate but actually develop in subtlety and vibrational level, just like everything else. The post-ascension world will not be unlike Atlantis, but will be lived more in the higher mental body rather than the third-chakra-astral-body desires for power and gratification. It will be a return to a golden age by adults, a definite upgrade, as you say now, on the adolescents of the previous round.

And, speaking of upgrades, we are expecting a significant qualitative increase in soul probe transmissions, as the vibrational increase aspect of the ascension process will inevitably bring them closer to us. Understanding of Monad's function and abilities will become more widespread, as the guarded secret of the ages grows through myth and rumour to raise its head above the late snows of spring. Call us foolish dreamers, call us irresponsible, but we believe it's about to happen. Finally, after all these millennia.

What about the millions of souls whose religious belief systems completely preclude any notion of Monads? Well, they know us under a number of names now: angels, deities, ancestral spirits, guides and so on and, of course, we are forced to work with them under the definitions they assume. After the process is complete, or more likely as it is unfolding, their unconscious definitions will be expanded, allowing us more, as you say, room to move.

Can we, as some of you are no doubt wondering, move forward through the illusion of time and see what the process will bring? Well certainly we can, but possible outcomes are what we see. We can always do this, and often do. But the futures we see are always fluid and full of options. Energy can travel down many paths as it winds its way back to what appears to be its source. When we look towards the end point of evolution on this planet we only see the beginning of a more cosmic evolutionary path; a graduation from Earth, followed by a graduation from the Milky Way, and so on. We need not remind you of the almost unimaginable vastness revealed by modern astronomy. Suffice to say that each one of those heavenly bodies light years away either is ensouled or has the potential to be so, and that Monads will do the ensouling, that is the shepherding of whatever sentient life-forms are envisioned and developed for the project. Will there be new 'young' Monads coming online that we will be training, as we once were? I think you know the answer to that.

14

CURRE

————➤●◄————

Currently, Gordon sees the por[ ] for this level of transmission. [ ] he needs to see, what he feels [ ] ters a sustained meditation he uncove[ ] and sees me as this undiscovered coun[ ] ly mapping. The purpose of this proje[ ] readers, into greater and deeper revelat[ ] another step in that direction now.

As 'I' focus on Gordon writing, I c[ ] (13), (15), and (16) all engaged in a sir[ ] thoughts into written language. Each [ ] a unique exploration of their mental [ ] to their character, cultural self-defini[ ] emotional issues, contributes a singu[ ] clopedia of understandings of the 'wri[ ] I can feel (17), (18), and (19), all of whor[ ] of a religious nature - (19) in copying a[ ] volvement all relates to the greater glory[ ] its unveiling. And to a lesser extent (14[ ] like (5), he is more concerned with the tr[ ] And tends to feel that the written word[ ] treachery in the realm of the sacred.

All these [ ] but the lear[ ] or prayer, h[ ] they are not[ ] or some rew[ ] tion, the de[ ] (16) underst[ ] a certain pr[ ] as their har[ ] stand the r[ ] and (14) are[ ] player, ben[ ] them. Havi[ ] to the grea[ ] inevitabilit[ ] volved in c[ ] actor recei[ ] contributed[ ] he benefits [ ] all time hig[ ]

Surely th[ ] chic space t[ ] limitless so[ ] both. He n[ ] Monad lea[ ] don' roam [ ] ty, and wh[ ] born? Or a[ ] I have ans[ ] He tells m[ ] lief system[ ] thing else [ ]

Is it the[ ] experimer[ ] the full ac[ ] the prolife[ ] feels it an[ ] (22) ha[ ] give an ac[ ] the key c[ ]

energy like children with colourful rubber balls. We loved the games we invented and played in the energetic pathways we opened. When Gordon feels his life opening up with almost endless possibilities and variations, as he does some mornings, he is catching the flavour of the energetic excitements which jangled nervous systems in Atlantis. Everything seemed possible; everything was possible. We were ambitious, we were giddy, we were silly. We were constantly tricking each other in ways you moderns might describe as magic or even black magic. The psychic attack and psychic self-defence mechanisms you are familiar with now were originated with us. Our motivations were altogether more mischievous than malicious however. That kind of nastiness in human affairs came later, as the dark ages of materialism and spiritual terror slowly took over. In our days power was more played with than lusted after, although one would have to admit the slide towards obsession with what you moderns would call the perks and privileges of position was well underway. For some, what began as a psychic chess game ended up as a war of pride and retribution.

Things got out of hand, to put it mildly. Devas that had been our playmates became, through callous misuse, vengeful rivals. Some thought we deserved what was coming to us and, instead of diverting the destructive repercussions of Mother Nature, as they might have done had our remorse been in any way palpable, they played their part with something resembling glee.

Some kind of end was approaching and those of us who were not in complete denial debated what its exact nature might be. As we watched and discussed, the far-sighted among us prepared ships to sail to the Mediterranean and the Americas, where colonies might be established and teachings earthed and transmitted. Many of us passed naturally before the final destruction and we helped prepare the way for the many who were to arrive in shock. A giant rescue and rehabilitation project ensued, in which we barely had time to feel the remorse and regret appropriate to our earlier misbehaviour. We were still children at heart, shunning our growth in Paradise. And, as such, we were models for much of the careless indulgences of later soul probes, who, when giving mere seconds of contemplation to some rash action justified in the heat of passion, would sense, subconsciously of course, their transgression to be tiny in the shadows of our catastrophic frivolities.

And wishing, finally, to assist in the transmission of the ancient wisdom in one of the cultures seeded by our farsighted members I descended with compatriots to Egypt where another round of lessons were to be convened by karma and its close associates.

15

AFTER EGYPT

After Egypt, where several incarnations can be summarized by
the experiences of the priest figure (13), a spiritual haven was
found in pre-Christian Britain and the Druidic culture there
existing. This was a place and time where man could exist in a friendly
but not hierarchic harmony with nature, where rivers, forests, valleys
and mountains were what we might now call community partners. A
place and time where the dynastic and power group struggles of Egypt
could be gratefully forgotten. A place where spirituality could be developed with a minimum of oppressive dogma and hidebound ritual.
A place where priests served the community and not the other way
around. A place where this aspect of 'Gordon' found a comfort zone
in which his ambitions could be fulfilled without threatening the desires of others.

In Egypt, after some trial runs, where apprenticeship to culture was
rivalled only by devotion to family, a life was given over to his notions
that God, or the God experience, could be accessed by the common
man without the intercession of the caste made up of his fellow priests.
He wanted man to know the joy and fulfilment of merging his mind
and heart with the deity who, he felt from his own explorations, encompassed the solar system with his being. While some, including the
Pharaoh, sympathised, many others, wishing to maintain their privi-
leged position, did not, and their machinations resulted in his torture

and downfall. His was an idea whose time had not yet come, but he knew that pioneers must plant their seeds in the soil of both personal and planetary suffering, so that the blooms of joy and serenity might blossom under more fortuitous conditions. In his soul he knew he was but a servant of the light, but in his ego he craved the prize of personal ambition realised, and his prideful downfall took some rest and recuperation time in spirit until he was ready to face his advisers, all of whom had given him prior warning of the recklessness of his enterprise.

But they had good news: communities and landscapes existed where his ambitions might be at least partially fulfilled. Druidism, as then practised, was more a brotherhood than a hierarchy and, once maturity had been attained, the individual practitioner was given free rein to pursue his individual path. Thus this aspect of 'Gordon' was able to introduce those seekers who came to him for guidance a measure of the greater mysteries then being promoted by another in his soul group in Ancient Greece. His method was a personally conducted initiation, facilitated by a herbal/mushroom concoction, not identical but yet not entirely dissimilar to those employed in the mass theatricals of the Greek mystery schools.

In sacred groves watched over by ancient oaks, pupils were raised beyond both the spirits of nature and the dead to the realm of radiance where *knowing* unfolded in an instant and seemingly without effort. Intractable problems were not so much resolved but understood and then dissolved. Mysteries melted, suffering ceased – at least for long enough to let the experiencer see how the Supreme Consciousness shuffled the cards of life so that the game could be played by multitudes with an infinitude of skills. 'Later' aspects (16) and (26) would experience similar illuminations in solitary meditation and emerge, not surprisingly, with their Buddhist and Christian conditioning supplying them with useful versions of the radiant void/godhead/ground of all consciousness.

As that fruitful incarnation unfolded, news of the teacher from the Mediterranean arrived on the shores of Albion. The Druid did not like what he heard and how he felt. They already had, he felt, an entirely suitable spiritual worldview, and did not require another from the land of sand and olive trees. He and some compatriots practised projecting the energies of repulsion, with somewhat less success than their descendants in 1940's England when the Nazi tide was seemingly and surprisingly turned upon Russia. 'I' – that is this aspect of Gordon writing – perceived this action quite vividly in meditation some years ago, and was even more curious later to perceive that 'earlier' aspect sitting down with his guides and advised, in no uncertain terms, to apply himself to harmonising with the Christ energy being rooted into the planet; to refrain from fighting it, whatever its manifestation. This polite lecture resulted in three, as far as 'I' can tell, lives in service to the Christian bureaucracy in dark ages and medieval Britain, between about 300 and 1400 AD, all three of which can be seen in summary in the life of (17). The life of (18), although Christian, was that of a contemplative monk, not a priest active in the community like the others, and actually more in sympathy with that of (26).

This reformed Druid, in all three of the 'service to the Christ impulse' lives, was never much more than a pagan in disguise, always secretly rebelling against the asceticism and self-punishment wrought by the overwhelming load of sinfulness larded onto believers by a church ever ready to enslave rather than liberate. And, of course, for many centuries, the peasants, fishers, and farmers of those isles were no more than nominally Christian anyway, their pagan relations with nature spirits and the land being the deep roots onto which their Latin reading re-organisers struggled mightily to plant saints and sinfulness.

These lads were just not buying the package. We were here to experience life in its fullness not repress it into the slavery of goodness and piety. At least one of them, and perhaps all three, pursued the secret path of sensuality, showing many an initially reluctant nun how pleasure need not result in pregnancy. He saw this aspect all too clearly, how man could serve woman without enslaving her. It would seem, to this Gordon, that this attitude, stemmed from the life of (14) and matured into that of (12), whose intimate understanding of the pleasures of life and flesh could be combined into a rapturous giving that was deserving of Divine Mother status.

(14), enabled by good looks, family status, and wealth, played like a faun in the fields of sensuality, enjoying all the pleasures such a life could bring, including the petty jealousies erupting amongst his favourites. Certainly vanity played a role in all of this, but its all-consuming power was held in check by a healthy sense of the ridiculous in all men, including himself. His playful pastimes found themselves reanimated in (21), whose absent, indulgent and later, conveniently dead husband, allowed her the freedom to play around with whomever caught her fancy, including a serving girl from the local village, whose husband later found her remarkably comfortable with his amorous intentions.

Playmates across the centuries these two, and 'I' can feel their influence on my own romantic escapades, although their level of sheer playfulness is, in 'me', somewhat restrained by an ever active probing intellect, the scholar easily outpacing the sensualist, and, to be truthful, often testing the patience of his partners.

Yet, by far the most accomplished in the ways of love and the good life was (12), from whom we have already heard. Quite devoted to all the arts of the courtesan, she could charm, enthrall, and seduce even the thorniest rose. In understanding fully, after some earlier lives, where lack of self-esteem and societal status allowed her to let in the energies of abuse and neglect, that catering to the needs of another was to be a ministering angel in the flesh, and that giving unstintingly of oneself, without a scintilla of reserve, was to let the energy of the universe flow through you and feed you simultaneously from the divine mother who nourishes all.

Her efforts have allowed 'me' to feel that divine mother energy pouring through 'me' as I perform the hands-on body healing that 'came to me' out of the blue in the early days of my healing practice. Although other streams of influence are pouring in, the Reiki energy for one, her warm massaging hands suffusing aching limbs and their more tender and generally unspoken counterparts, play a not insignificant role. Her love for faltering, insecure humanity, informs the voice which conveys aspects of the ancient wisdom in my seminars. And although 'Gordon's' balance of animus and anima comes from many sources and earlier less-than-successful experiments, the bulk of it streams directly from her, and for all that I give thanks. When I am confident, relaxed and giving in human relations, it's largely because of her. When I act from insecurity, self-doubt and fears, 'I' am feeling the influence of (10) and, to a lesser extent (11), (19), and (20). (10), thankfully for the rest of us, explored the depths of self-loathing, paranoia, and despair so well that we were spared the grim exercise, although not the bottom-of-the-barrel vibrations cascading through us when we touch the fringes of that despair in ourselves. When 'I' have been lost and am full of self-crucifying doubts and angers, it is her painful wandering and demise I am channelling. When 'I' feel cast aside carelessly or ruthlessly abandoned, it is the hopeless insecurities of (11) and (20) I'm feeling and, to a lesser extent (19), whose abandonment was cushioned by status, money, and the blessing of male progeny. (11) and (20) lost it all, as we say. Their pathos and despair are as eternal as any joy or bliss coming from other sources and can be dipped into at will almost anytime. We learn from the dark and the light. Watch yourself as you run from pain and into the arms of pleasure: it is an intriguing exercise. Most of us do it on an almost daily basis. I am not suggesting you employ other, more elevated, motivations, but I am inferring that there is much to learn from observing the human bouncing about. Seeing yourself as the toy of desire and fear as well as the prime mover of your incarnation is to understand yourself as pawn and king, and that alone is worth the price of entry.

Reminder:

Gordon, "I", whom you know:

1. A king, circa 1570-1630
2. A philosopher, circa 1700-1770
3. Another philosopher, 1300's
4. A Druid priest figure, circa 20 B.C. - 30 A.D.
5. A Celtic chieftain of the middle ages
6. A small time businessman in ancient China
7. A wife and mother in ancient China
8. A trader in Holland, circa 1600-1650
9. A young girl, dead at around five, circa 1900
10. An outcast, selling herself to survive, England circa 1730
11. A wife awaiting the return of her husband from sea
12. A wealthy and influential Venetian courtesan, circa 1550
13. A member of the priestly caste under Ahkenaten in Egypt
14. An artistically inclined son of a wealthy Athenian family, bisexual
15. A lesser-known member of the Neoplatonist school
16. A contemplative monk in England, circa 1300
17. An abbot of a monastery, circa 1400
18. An Irish monk, circa 700
19. A daughter of high birth, left pregnant while husband goes to war 1650?
20. Also an archetype for 11 young wife who lost her husband at sea, circa 1880.
21. A French noblewoman with an inherited estate, bisexual playgirl, circa 1780
22. An Atlantean male, steeped in magical energy work, yet carefree and completely without the ego attachments of those who engaged in the 'magical workings' of more recent times.

23. & 24. A woman and a man, fairly primitive, brutal 'Viking Raider' types
25. Minor Scottish noble, impoverished, circa 1250
26. Buddhist monk (India/Tibet/Nepal) circa 1000

16

RESTING IN PEACE

It is quite peaceful here, but perhaps not quite as peaceful as folks would wish for their dear departed. You can, once you are over the stresses of transition and the excitements of the 'welcome home' parties, select a remote country cottage set in some verdant valley with the requisite number of fields, streams, forests and friendly wildlife, move in and begin your rest in earnest. It works. It works so well, in fact, that you will tire of it before you know it. And thanks to the telepathic communication and instant (or almost instant) teleportation, friends, relatives, colleagues, pleasure, fun, amusing diversions and stimulating courses are all at your fingertips. And the more you avail yourself the more you want to avail yourself. Apart from those of us traumatised by the cruelties of war, famine, or disease, who take their time recovering, we all slide all too easily into the amazing breadth of activity here in the post-mortem world. It's you on Earth who want us to rest in peace; we, here, tend to play in varying degrees of gratification, pleasure, and joy. But as the divide between our worlds is still large enough to support these traditional illusions, we forgive you!

There are those here who relate mostly to others they are connected to from their most recent incarnation. It does not occur to them that they might interact with those they knew from five hundred years ago, or longer. But they can. If an aspect of Higher Self/Monad, as every in-carnation is, or a soul probe, as some call it, has completed its journey down through the planes and then back up reuniting with its source, its Monad, it can be contacted and consulted for your general edifica-tion and, dare I say it, fun! These historical personalities are real, live sentient beings, who will communicate the essence of their character and epoch. In meditation from where you are now, they can be experi-enced as holographic data files, movies come to life as soon as you en-ter their aura, or otherwise plead at the door of their being, but when you are fully in spirit and ready to reach beyond the astral paradise that many of your contemporaries will still think of as 'home', you can ascend to the Monadic plane and interact with as many of these com-pleted personalities as you can handle.

For 'Gordon' you have already been introduced to the group he feels are most influential on his incarnational formation and current pro-gress. Hopefully you can extrapolate this into your own incarnational history and see, with not too much straining of whatever belief system you treasure, that 'you', as an extension of your Higher Self/Monad, are intimately connected to all the other extensions – variations on a theme, to use a musical analogy – and, as such, have representatives of yourself in most, if not exactly every, epoch and culture, and are, in essence, history. *You are history.*

And that is, more or less, the point. The Monad extends itself en-ergetically to all forms of nature, all forms of animal, plant, mineral, and all the permutations of human personality and endeavour. When the personalities learn all the lessons, reap all their karma, and have all their fun, and that is added to the cache of mineral, plant, animal experiences, the Monad is completed, its data banks overflowing, and is ready to graduate from what some have called the Earth Life Sys-tem. This is, not surprisingly, a long way from resting in peace. But then again, even those who have recently transitioned and are enjoy-ing their long holiday in Paradise or Heaven have jettisoned that se-rene sojourn for the joys of play and learning. It's only those still on Earth who wish to rest in peace. And, given the exhausting hurly-burly of daily life, who can blame them? As for me, Mr. Monad, I rest in the perpetually shifting poise of bliss.

17

YOU ARE HISTORY

Gordon loves to study history, its subtle complexities of class, culture, religion, diplomacy, and militarism enthralling him every time he opens a book or watches a documentary. Despite seeing behaviour patterns repeated ad infinitum by individuals and societies, he feels he is learning the infinite subtleties and variations contained in those patterns and, in the process, is becoming something of an expert in a field neither appreciated nor named in the halls of academe. He's thinking maybe 'Soul Growth, Societal Transformation and The Earth Project' might be a start. He feels this book, among others of its type, will be a small contribution.

He is seeing himself, this current version of his Higher Self's mutability, as an actor in the unfolding costume drama of history, and all the 'past' as other roles in earlier acts. As he focuses, from time to contemplative time, on these other roles, and feels their psychic influences on his own patterns, he feels he is a living part of history; that history as well as something you study, is something *that you are*. In deep meditation, when he can sink into the fears, joys, anxieties, stresses, puzzlements, and fevered pursuits of those others, he can see they are all one; one audacious experiment in humanity, one miniscule thread in the tapestry, one magical theme with many variations, all of which were admirable efforts under the circumstances, strained this way and that by the desires and fears of others.

In deep meditation he can also see that all human beings are variations on the one human, personalities acting out the ambitions and fears apparently bred in the bone, but maybe also picked out from a prearranged and eagerly proffered palette, sometimes attaining results and occasionally resolutions. He can also see the chains of cause and effect stretching through the centuries, the ripples reaching the shore many lives after the stone was thrown. He can feel himself simultaneously caught in the pattern and yet ever morphing into new designs; designs which challenge the perception into mapping the differences and similarities, and then laugh at the ever-so-temporary results. It is a sobering and yet elevating experience and Gordon would like all his readers to have it for themselves.

If this text does not accomplish that, then perhaps some accompanying exercises might tip the balance; that balance which allows us to be sociable citizens, our neuroses carefully in check; that balance which can be skewed away from self and its self-consciousness out into the cosmos of many selves all sharing the light as they look for it.

Yes, that is what Gordon would like.

18

THE MONAD, AS OFFERED BY OTHERS

———— ✦ ————

lthough "I" am a Monad, a Higher Self whom you would all like to honour, who can operate the levers of my being like no other, Gordon suspects that the views of other recent incarnates, although more partial than complete, would aid the reader in realising some of her ambitions. The following is what he's finding:

> The Monad is a drop out of the shoreless ocean beyond, or, to be correct, within the plane of primeval differentiation. It is divine in its higher, and human in its lower condition (the adjectives 'higher' and 'lower' being used for lack of better words), and a Monad remains, at all times, save in the Nirvanic state, under whatever conditions, or whatever external forms. As the Logos reflects the Universe in the Divine Mind, and the manifested Universe reflects itself in each of its Monads (as Leibnitz put it when repeating an Eastern teaching), so the Monad has, during the cycle of its incarnations, the ability to reflect itself in every root form of each kingdom. Therefore the Kabbalists

say correctly that "Man becomes a stone, a plant, an animal, a man, a spirit, and finally God. Thus accomplishing his cycle or circuit and returning to the point from which he had started as the heavenly Man". But by 'Man', the divine Monad is meant, and not the thinking entity, much less his physical body.

That's Helena Blavatsky from her masterwork *The Secret Doctrine.*

So we used such expressions as 'looking up to the higher self', 'listening to the promptings of the higher self', and so on. I remember that Mr. Sinnett used sometimes to speak a little disparagingly of the higher self, remarking that it ought to take more interest than it seemed to do in the unfortunate personality struggling on its behalf down here; and he used jokingly to suggest the formation of a society for the education of our higher selves. It was only gradually that we grew into the feeling that the higher self was the man, and that what we see down here is only a very small part of him. Only little by little did we learn that there is only one consciousness, and that the lower, though an imperfect representation of the higher, is in no way separate from it. We used to think of raising 'ourselves' till we could unite ourselves with that glorified higher being', not realizing that it was the higher that was the true self, and that to unite the higher to the lower really meant opening out the lower so that the higher might work in it and through it.

That's Charles Leadbeater from *The Monad and Other Essays.* And further, from the same book:

There is the Monad, the Divine Spark, which is verily a fragment of God, an atom of the Deity. Crude and inaccurate expressions, assuredly; yet I know of no other way in which the idea can be conveyed even as well as in words such as these. For each Monad is literally part of God, apparently temporarily separated from him, while he is enclosed in the veils of matter, though in truth never for one moment really separated. He can never be apart from God, for the very matter in which he veils himself is also a manifestation of the Divine. To us sometimes matter seems evil, because it weighs us down, it clogs our faculties, it seems to hold us back upon our road; yet remember that this is only because as yet we have not learned to control it, because we have not realized that it is also divine in its essence, because there is nothing but God.

And how about Alice Bailey, in her long unwinding of the thought of "the Tibetan", the ascended master who offered his teachings through her pen during the decades 1920-60.

> *Monad*: The One. The threefold spirit on its own plane. In occultism it often means the unified triad – Atma Buddhi, Manas; Spiritual Will, Intuition and Higher Mind – or the immortal part of man which reincarnates in the lower kingdoms, and gradually progresses through them and thence to the final goal.

That's from her first book *Initiation, Human and Solar.*

And how about this, from *Discipleship In The New Age, Vol.2.:*

> The Monad is the source of light, not only to the human family, but it is the receiver of light from the threefold sun; it is the lens through which the light of the solar Logos can flow to the planetary Logos, preserving and holding steady in that light the vision, the purpose, the will and the creative intention of the planetary Logos.

Finally, from this source, at least for now, there is this, from *A Treatise on Cosmic Fire:*

> The evolution of the Monad is a much more intricate thing than appears in the books as yet given to the public. In those books the development of consciousness and its transition through the kingdoms of nature are the points dwelt upon. Yet there have been earlier cycles, which it will only be possible to comprehend as the history and evolution of the planetary Logoi become gradually revealed.

And...

> The Monad has cycles analogous, though on a miniature scale, to those of the One Life who permeates and animates all lesser lives. Certain of these cycles cover periods of time so vast, and so long past, that their history can only be conveyed to the investigating adepts through the medium of sound and symbol."

And again, from Leadbeater's *The Monad*

We may reverently presume that when we have finally and fully realized that the Monad is the true man, we shall find behind that again and yet further a more glorious extension; we shall find that the Spark has never been separated from the Fire, but that as the ego (higher self) stands behind the personality, as the Monad stands behind the ego, so a Planetary Angel stands behind the Monad, and the Solar Deity himself stands behind the Planetary Angel. Perhaps, even further still, it may be that in some way infinitely higher, and so at present utterly incomprehensible, a greater Deity stands behind the Solar Deity, and behind even that, through many stages, there must rest the Supreme over all."

"For the time, at least, the Monad is our personal God, the god within us, that which produces us down here as a manifestation of him on these all but infinitely lower levels.

Christopher M. Bache's *Lifecycles* (1990), continues some of these overtly Theosophical themes for the modern reader. He uses, as do others these days, the term 'Oversoul', and his definition, "the larger consciousness that incorporates and integrates all the experiences gathered in our many incarnations" connects most comfortably with the Monad described as above.

While the Oversoul's knowledge and power seem extraordinary, it appears to focus its attention on helping us learn what we have come to earth to learn. We are the means through which it is now learning what it must learn to complete itself. It completes itself by helping us complete ourselves. We are its current student in the Earth school, a part of itself sent off to work for the good of the whole, yet obliged to forget its tie to the whole as part of the conditions of learning. And yet this forgetfulness can be penetrated to a degree even while we are in the Earth school. Once we know of the existence of the Oversoul and of our connection to it, we can begin to open ourselves to it in a deeper way. We can, to a degree, make an unconscious relationship conscious.

Later he comes very close to the *You Are History* theme:

Reincarnation gives us reasons to ask larger questions about what we are and what our place in the scheme of things is. It also gives us cause to expect larger answers to these questions. When we begin to glimpse our true longevity, when we begin to appreciate the true scope of our lives, we can no longer see ourselves as simply the citizens of one country or one century. We must instead come to see ourselves as time travelers with unrestricted passports. It is not our present ego-personality that reaches this far across time, but the Oversoul. The Oversoul is our bridge into the cosmos. Our place in the Divine Order is through its life and work. Through our participation in it we become part of the processes stretching across eons of time; processes so vast that we must struggle to see even the possibilities.

Jane Roberts preferred the term 'source self', and, taking a break from channeling her famous Seth books, explored its reality in the book *Adventures In Consciousness* (1975):

The source self is the fountainhead of our present physical being, but it exists outside of that frame of reference. We are earth versions of ourselves, beautifully tuned into corporal experience. Our known consciousness is filtered through perceptive mechanisms that are part of what they perceive. We are the instruments through which we know the earth.

In other terms we are particles of energy, flowing from the source self into physical materialization. Each source self from many such particles, or 'Aspect Selves' that impinge upon three dimensional reality, striking our space-time continuum. Others are not physical at all, but have their existence in completely different systems of reality. Each Aspect Self is connected to the other, however, through the common experience of the source self, and can to some degree draw on the knowledge, abilities and perceptions of the other Aspects."

"Psychologically, these other aspects appear within the known self as personality traits, characteristics, and talents that are uniquely ours. The individual is the particle or focus personality, formed by the intersection of the unknown self, or at least to a recognition of its existence. I believe that we can also use the Aspects of this source self within us to expand our conscious knowledge and experience.

Bruce Moen, in his *Exploring The Afterlife* series, touched on the Higher Self several times. In Volume Four, *Voyage To Curiosity's Father*, he states:

> For me, Oversoul, Disk, I/There, Greater Self, Higher Self are all words used to describe the same thing. Previous explorations have led me to believe I exist as the individual expression of myself. I see this Oversoul, or Disk, a version of me viewing reality from a much broader perspective within the Whole of consciousness.

Later in conversation with a spirit being he calls CW (Consciousness Worker) he hears:

> The Disk/Oversoul is a separate thing from ELS (Earth Life System), exploring the Great Unknown to bring what it finds there into the awareness of consciousness. Your Disk is focused within that portion of the Great Unknown called the Earth Life System. Its members inhabit all levels of this system, and gather into the Disk all of its unknowns."

Some members of the Disk have spent their entire existence as CW's, workers in the various centers of Focus 27. These members have never experienced lifetimes within physical reality. They are gathering details of the operation of the nonphysical, control center portion of the ELS. They are exploring the infrastructure of the thought form side of the ELS. Some Disk members are exploring other thought form sides of the ELS within various levels such as Focus levels 22 through 26. Other Disk members are cycling through lifetimes within physical reality on Earth, gaining knowledge of that side of the ELS. Still other members of the Disk are exploring the ELS connections to other schools outside the ELS; alien worlds you might call them.

The Disk members, who have completed exploration of their area of the Unknown within the ELS, can be considered its permanent members, or, the Disk itself. Permanent in this context means they no longer cycle through physical or non-physical lifetimes, nor do they experience separation from each other. They remain continuously, consciously aware, as a unified portion of the whole being that includes both the Disk and Off-Disk members. In this context, Off-Disk members are still those cycling through lifetimes within various realities. The Disk maintains awareness of all portions of the ELS via filament of awareness connections to all Off-Disk members. Together the Disk and all Off-Disk members are a single, unified, conscious, self-aware Being."

...Since the Disk is connected to all Off-Disk members, it has direct access to all knowledge gathered by them. The Disk serves as a storage repository of all such knowledge, as well as the means for interactively sharing this knowledge with all Off-Disk members.

And later when he asks, what 'graduation' may mean for a Disk, the answer does not come in words but in images and feelings:

"I experienced a sensation of expansion into space, as if I, as a Disk, was expanding to fill space. ..." As a graduated Disk I could create any life forms, planets, suns or environments I chose to include in my creation. I could create an Earth-like planet with carbon-based life-forms, or any other I chose. I could include a physical world lifetime cycle or modify it to a pure thought-form-based existence, or anywhere in between. Whatever choices I made in the creation of my system would be my choices.

And to come full circle in the now of 2013, let us repair to Ian Lawton's study *Supersoul*.

Replacing the terms Higher Self, Monad, Source etc., with his preference Supersoul, he muses: "Indeed we've seen that as supersouls we create whole worlds and universes ourselves, and doesn't that make us quite divine enough without us having to look any further? He continues, "Soul consciousness is holographic. We are both individual aspects of our supersoul, and full holographic representations of it, all at the same time. However this does not mean that soul individuality is in itself an illusion. The principle of the hologram is that the part contains the whole, and yet is clearly distinguishable from it."

And his formal definition is as follows:

A supersoul is a grouping of hundreds, maybe thousands, of souls. Myriads of supersouls are projecting soul aspects of themselves into this and myriad other realities, meaning they are very far from the ultimate consciousness. Yet to be fully connected to your supersoul is to have boundless wisdom and creative power, and as a full holographic representation of it you are already more divine than you can hope to conceive – divine enough, even, to nullify further speculation about what beyond.

19

A SPRINKLING
OF SUGGESTIVE
EXERCISES

E xercise One: *Climbing the antahkarana like a ladder.*

As defined by esoteric teachings and understood by Gordon, the antahkarana is a column of light connecting the Monad through the various bodies (Monadic, Buddhic, Causal, Mental, Astral) down into the incarnate personality, a connection which exists initially as a trickle but can be strengthened by the conscious practice of meditation and visualisation.

As you follow the energy moving upwards from your crown chakra through the increasing increments of vibration which admits the explorer through the various levels and sub-levels of the spiritual dimensions, you can encounter elementals, nature spirits, garden fairies, landscape devas, the entire panoply of the 'dead'; that ever shifting population of discarnate souls in the various stages of shaking off their Earth based trials and traumas, embracing the rewards of Paradise and joys of Heaven, the formless and blissfully inscrutable energy realms beyond the heavens of love and devotion, leading to that sea of bliss, that radiant void wherein the Monads move and have their being. Once there, however you conceive or experience it, you can merge and meet up with any and all of your 'soul family', feeling out whatever aspects of their journeys you find acceptable or believable as your doubts and lack of worth play out their usual games.

As with all spiritual exercise, regular practice deepens the experience. Begin in the home, with calm and quiet as your companions. Save the pleasant gardens and favoured nature spots until later, as the beauties of your surroundings can be distracting until you have settled into the inner serenity necessary.

Exercise Two: Asking your guides.

Assuming that you have already made more than an initial contact to bring one or other of your soul family members for a visit, so when they 'arrive', adjust your meditation to telepathic conversation. This is for those of you who prefer the passive role, who feel that travel, albeit of the energetic variety, is not for you. As you move through these interviews, the various epochs, societies, religions, and family dynamics, will, to one degree or another, resonate with your own journey and you will begin to fathom a depth of interaction, in terms of issues and challenges, that your soul family presents. There will be times, of course, when you suspect you're merely nattering away to yourself, and wish to hide the practice from prying eyes, but do persevere and you will find your confidence growing in leaps and bounds as the concept of 'you' deepens and widens to include the details of other dramas, somehow foreign and familiar at the same time.

Exercise Three: Examining the various character archetypes in your local community.

Every neighbourhood and town has its 'characters', some of them strangers, some of them acquaintances, some of them friends. Need I enumerate them? The embattled single mom, the confident career woman, the self-pitying widow, the overbearing interfering grandmother, the man-killing glamour girl, the nervous Nellie scared of her own shadow, the hardworking shop owner, the ruthless businessman, the middle management warrior, the handsome devil, the sports nut, the functioning alcoholic, the doper on death's doorstep, the retired professional reaping the benefits, the frail elderly, the pious and sanctimonious, the anxious breeders of babies, and so on.

Examine them all, slowly, carefully, empathetically; see what motivates their behaviours, both neurotic and much approved, their concept of citizenship, their habits and affectations, their unconscious assumptions and expectations. As you observe and take note, watch your reactions, for they will reveal much of your own issues, your own habitations of such character types in one or more past lives. Most of us have been here many thousands of years, each time thinking we were just us doing our bit and then dying. Now we know we were not merely one person but many, and each with equal value regardless of contemporary societal status. And don't forget, after the chess game both the king and the pawn go back in the box.

We are all actors constantly changing roles in the dramas, comedies, mysteries, and thrillers. We have starring roles, supporting roles, and cameo appearances. Sometimes we are extras standing around with nothing to say. Sometimes we are the script writer and director all in one. Sometimes we take our direction from others with their own stories to enact. Sometimes the drama is so tragic we can't take it. Sometimes the comedy is so funny we can't stand it. Sometimes the mystery is so perplexing we leave the stage as befuddled as when we arrived. But each time the movie is archived for later use. There's thousands upon thousands of them in the Akashic Records, as you may have already heard. Many of them are quite similar in the unfolding of their behaviour patterns, but the minor variations make them intriguing to the participants. And that brings us back to character archetypes.

20

MORE SOUL PROBES

R *eminder:*

Gordon, "I", whom you know:

1. A king, circa 1570-1630
2. A philosopher, circa 1700-1760
3. Another philosopher, 1300's
4. A Druid priest figure, circa 20 B.C. - 30 A.D.
5. A Celtic chieftain of the middle ages
6. A small time businessman in ancient China
7. A wife and mother in ancient China
8. A trader in Holland, circa 1600-1650
9. A young girl, dead at around five, circa 1900
10. An outcast, selling herself to survive, England circa 1730
11. A wife awaiting the return of her husband from sea
12. A wealthy and influential Venetian courtesan, circa 1550
13. A member of the priestly caste under Ahkenaten in Egypt
14. An artistically inclined son of a wealthy Athenian family, bisexual
15. A lesser-known member of the Neoplatonist school
16. A contemplative monk in England, circa 1300

17. An abbot of a monastery, circa 1400
18. An Irish monk, circa 700
19. A daughter of high birth, left pregnant while husband goes to war 1650?
20. Also an archetype for 11, young wife who lost her husband at sea, circa 1880.
21. A French noblewoman with an inherited estate, bisexual playgirl, circa 1780
22. An Atlantean male, steeped in magical energy work, yet carefree and completely without the ego attachments of those who engaged in the 'magical workings' of more recent times
23. & 24. A woman and a man, fairly primitive, brutal 'Viking Raider' types
25. Minor Scottish noble, impoverished, circa 1250
26. Buddhist monk (India/Tibet/Nepal) circa 1000

Continuing our exploration deeper into the energetic exchange between Gordon and his cast of characters, he finds himself recalling the many years of dream recall, back in the awakening period when he thought such work was only for him, wherein 'he' would be assisting and encouraging a variety of characters who were fighting oppression and injustice, showing them more of the cunning, duplicity, and risk-taking bravery necessary to their tasks. Some were rebels of a political stripe, some were outlaws as defined by the power structure, some were heretics to the reigning belief system, some were fighting enslavement, but all required the sudden wild inspirations which feed the well of courage.

These years of intermittent dream recall took place in decades where he actively believed in past lives but had only uncovered one or two of his own and had not thought to connect behaviours and attitudes through time. But once he had begun to assemble his 'cast of characters' through the various portals of entry into his ever expanding consciousness, he began to see the life of (5), a minor Scottish/Celtic chieftain embroiled in the decades' long struggle to rid Scotland of its English occupiers, as a major influence in several areas, not the least of which was the courage, unwavering determination, evasiveness and cunning necessary to lengthy guerilla warfare. Finally he connected these dream recalls of subversion and cunning evasion of corrupt authority, helping characters from many epochs and societies, to this source. He also sees his habit of eating quickly

when alone as a remnant of that man's on-the-run lifestyle, a habit hard to lose when he's dining with friends! Yet such is the matrix
of influences this is modified by the more sophisticated and luxu-
rious dining habits of (2), (12) and (1), particularly (2) and (12), who
took great pleasure in providing meals and entertainment for close
friends. Gordon has come to the point in his exercise of the observer
consciousness where he can see the multiple influences streaming in
one after the other, blending themselves almost seamlessly into the
polished enigma he is now.

When Gordon ponders his keen interest in Scotland's 2014 independence referendum, he can feel not only his own pride in sovereign-
ty regained, but the triumphant howl of 'freedom at last' from (5). (1)
is also pleased at the prospect, or at least its possibility, as he feels the
Great Britain experiment is almost over and the European 'unity in
diversity' stage is an idea whose time has most definitely come. And
(2), with some reservations, seems to agree. His reservations appear to
come from his study of alien civilisations visiting Earth. Their claims
of colonisation notwithstanding, he considers the Galactic Federation
option to be of more challenge and relevance. In making this point he
feels to be somewhat shy and self-effacing, at least to Gordon, who suspects he does not care to be seen as 'stepping on toes'. It is Gordon's
book after all. Gordon smiles, knowing not only authorial pride from
the inside, but also his indebtedness to (2)'s pioneering work, both in
philosophical clarity and stylistic elegance. (2) is not the only writer
in Gordon's soul family. There are several others, notably (1), (3), (12)
and (15). Their cumulative effect is to make the craft of literary composition second nature in Gordon. As he lives he breathes and writes.

When Gordon is brought low by the prospect of economic difficulties that look like disasters in the making, he tunes into the energy
stream from (25), whose gradual impoverishment brought neglect onto
his tenants and servants and the shame of eviction onto him. When
he feels lonely, neglected, and depressed he knows he is harmonising
with the hopelessness and depression of (10), whose scouring of the
bottom-of-the-barrel in self-loathing became a touchstone not only
for Gordon but for all the others in the group.

When he is angry and rebellious at the authorities of organised religion, he knows he is channelling the resentment of (3) who was forced
to travel hundreds of miles, some of it by foot, to defend his philosophical writings to the papal authorities then in Avignon and the iconoclastic rebelliousness of (13), who would not submit to the designs of

the power hungry priesthood and was tortured for his stance. And he would not deny the secondhand pleasure he now feels from the energetic input from (17), whose deftly hidden paganism subverted the various wrongheaded ideals of the Christianity as then practised.

Both (17) and the two earlier, but unnumbered, efforts to serve the Christ impulse, found their consummation, finally devoid of anarchic individualism, in (16) and (18), both contemplative monks, one English one Irish, whose hard-won inner stillness combines with that of (15) and (26) to fuel Gordon's own blessed interludes of serenity in his busy mechanised modernity.

(14) and (15) represent a fascinating polarity for Gordon. Both ancient Greeks, one an artsy bisexual hedonist and the other a lesser-known philosopher of the Neo-Platonist school, seem to Gordon the twin thrusts of action and contemplation, reverberating down through the centuries into (8) and (21), (21) having no qualms about indulging herself when the fancy took her and (8) hard-working, devoted to family and religion, but tying himself in knots over an extra-marital affair and punishing himself with a drowning.

Obviously (14) morphed into (8), exploring much the same territory from the other gender's perspective, and (15) made a brave attempt to bring his measure of the enlightenment made famous by the Neo-Platonist school into the world of (8), the Dutch trader, but only partially succeeding, as the mental conventionality of (8) trimmed down (15)'s broad horizons into devotion and duty serving exterior causes. And perhaps guilt, channelled unconsciously of course, from the fates of (11) and (19), whose men left them high and dry with babies to care for.

Gordon himself feels the fate of (19) keenly, as at least one of his own romantic disappointments seemed to have been engineered by (19)'s then partner, and more recently connected to him, whose sense of adventure outstripped their sense of commitment. In this betrayal he felt not only hurt and anger but vibe of karmic retribution for a violent incident in the life of (25) many centuries before, when he, as an impoverished and angry husband, kicked the swelling belly of his wife, denying her motherhood. Karma is, of course, a complex series of interactions across time, which can be speeded up, delayed and manifested with considerably more subtlety than the eye-for-an-eye iteration. Gordon also recognises that the cause and effect ping-pong, which karma represents, is actually a series of pre-birth choices made by the incarnating soul with the advice of guides and the input of other souls thus connected.

The bitter, rancid emotions of these various tragedies and betrayals mean little to Gordon now, although in their day they certainly stung. He recognises their usefulness, both in the exercise of fiery feelings and the scorching they provided to old and outworn structures. As fresh growth leaps out and up from the charred forest, so too does renewed impulse flutter free from the nets of self-pity.

Self-indulgence is a useful balance to self-pity and Gordon can see it quite clearly in (14) (12) and especially (21), who seems to have inherited (12)'s innate sensuality without its compensating empathy and compassion. (21) seems to have experienced satiety without much satisfaction, taking to an early death when her looks failed her. Still, she now says, she was an example to all around her, a fun loving sprite without the moral compunctions imposed on others by convention and religion. She feels that, although she ostensibly led that life for the pleasures of self-gratification, it was more for the benefit of hard-working others who could take vicarious pleasure in her carefree nose-thumbing antics. Consciously selfish but unconsciously selfless.

As "I" recount these issues and interrelationships I am simultaneously a mouthpiece broadcasting achievements and a shy, retiring schoolteacher, letting my charges speak for themselves, knowing that, when the class graduates, "I" do too. As I expand in my being, with sparks from my fire in all areas and all life forms of the Earth Life System and some elsewhere in the universe, being *extraterrestrial biological entities* with agendas seemingly all their own, I check in on everyone from 'time to time', observing their progress, their problem solving capabilities, their alignment with the universal energy that some call love, others quantum entanglement and others the grace of God, their ability to feel, think, act and trace their roots to source and see 'me' for what I am and not what they project, I come to know myself as a progenitor with many dependants all of whom think they're independent. And that is one of many paradoxes I live with bemusedly in your terms. I say your terms as that fits your comfort zone, whereas my high energy blissful contentment is far beyond it; the words I use are mere shadows in the radiance I exchange gifts with.

The above may only poeticise my being rather than explain it, as many of you may wish. Try to feel me as your source, an expanded version of you that has no form but can take on any form at will. A version that can be human, non-human, angelic, demonic, animal, plant or mineral. A magical being? Yes, by some standards, but a magical being with a commitment to the imprisonment of life in form, for that constriction is the source of knowledge and the wisdom distilled from it. That constriction from which all your notions of suffering emerges is not only the condition of your being but the tool from which you carve your release. I am not constricted, I only experience that through my extensions, like you. When you come to me with all your wisdom distilled from the tears of sadness and joy, the regrets, remorse, shame, and contrition resolved into thoughtful memories and symbols which I can easily absorb and later use, I am what you would call grateful and full of the loving kindness you all aspire to. Something akin, Gordon suggests, to a mother whose brood has returned, dirty and full of chatter, from a picnic in the park. Gordon also suggests that this is precisely what (12) encompassed in her exploration and made available to what he calls 'the rest of us'. Did she learn that from 'me'? I'd say she absorbed it and relayed it successfully despite having to swim upstream against the flow of selfish anxiety and ruthless ambition that clients brought to her door.

Need I remind you that all of you emanate from one or another Monad and encompass portions of Monadic consciousness in your humanity? I mention it at this point as you may be becoming enraptured with the dramatic details of Gordon's cast of characters and forgetting that you, despite both your doubts and curiosity, are a fully-fledged member of your own group soul/Monad. You too can trace the energetic beams full of thought and emotion crisscrossing the dimensions in precisely the same manner as Gordon has outlined for his cast of characters. *You*, in all your self-effacing searching, *Are History*. You are the peasant and the aristocrat, the farmer and the soldier, the mother and the child, the servant and the master, the priest and the nun, the monk and the abbot, the gambler and the drunk, the hawker and the customer, the chef and the served, the abuser and the abused.

Feel your way into each of their dreams; let them wash over you and cover you with connections. Let the links enliven you, move you out of your shell and into the other. The other who is you while both of you are me.

21

SIGNIFICANT
OTHERS

Your significant others are many and make you what you are, today or any other day.

You will see them as you explore what you thought was just
for others. Take note of their contribution. The makeup of your psyche
is mapped with contributions. You are uniquely you but also a conglomerate of inputs: a unique conglomerate of inputs from the vast
acres of space and time.

Realise that as you are constantly receiving energetic beams from
them, trapped as they might seem in the narrow confines of their existence, they are also receiving much the same from you, who, in compar-
ison, is a pampered princeling with many of the options of the modern
world at your fingertips. When they dream of a better life, of freedom
from family, society, and religion, it is fantasies dreamily derived from
your labour-saving and carefree Paradise which inspires them. When
you look to the future, perhaps wishing for a disease, war, and political
repression-free world, you are reaching into the energies unconsciously received from your future selves, whose experience of the higher vibration then common to their worlds uplifts you.

Gordon tries not to think of his future self, Cassiopeia – contacted
during the composition of *More Adventures In Eternity* – as her life seems

so magical and wearies him to cope with his. Not to mention how her existence seems to transgress his dearly held notions of free will. That he seems to be predestined to become her, after some suitable retooling of the psyche of course, offends his choice-loving self. Surely she is just one of several possible futures? And does that imply her parents have also been selected? From Gordon's viewpoint, no, but from Higher Self's viewpoint yes. And how are those viewpoints to be reconciled? By Gordon rising to the height of Higher Self and viewing all of the valley below, which also includes all his past selves, all his comrades in arms, and the choices he thought he was making between incarnations. Higher Self sees those choices manifested but does not relay that information to the reincarnating soul, precisely so that soul can work uninterruptedly with its guides and soul-mates and come up, through debate and compromise, with the next step in its spiritual evolution. Higher Self observes these stages bemusedly, even the disastrous ones, taking centuries to unravel their stupidity, knowing that whatever choice is cemented into physical reality the experiential information will make its unique contribution to the big picture; the big picture being the Monadic hotel transcending time and space, with its many settled inhabitants and newer arrivals, all ready for action in spheres beyond.

There is another future self that Gordon has sensed and written about: himself at the end of time; or to be more accurate, a modified version of himself – or herself if you include Cassiopeia and the other ladies in the group. He feels this ascending intelligence gazing at him from time to time, lovingly absorbing his various predicaments, most of which he assumes must feel quite primitive, and, of course they do, but no more than say (23) and (24) seem to him. Gordon senses this being to be an androgynous, barely physical, partly angelic time traveller, and in this he would not be far off the mark. The physical plane in that being's epoch is the Paradise that is the inevitable result of the merging of the astral and physical planes; a place where the so-called living and the so-called dead intermingle freely and ascension to the formless energy planes is available to any incarnate willing to surrender their beloved personality and make the leap to non-being. Gordon knows that this can be achieved now, in his epoch, but only in the out of body state, and only by those who are adventurous enough to give it a try, of which there are not many, attachment to character being what it is. He knows because astral aspects of 'him' participate in such exercises, using his 'cottage in f27' (see *More Adventures in Eternity*) as a base to launch from.

And in this, not surprisingly, he can see the current version of 'him' heading towards completion, however many decades or centuries it takes. In the tough times – in those mini dark nights of the soul, when the spirit seems stymied by the gravity of the past and its less-than-wise choices – such connective tissues are life-savers. Stumbling through the rough terrain of the valley, all bruised and bleeding, and seeing the alpine valley with its masses of wild flowers beckoning in the sunshine, can be just what the doctor ordered.

22

MORE MOVIES

On occasion, during the long winter evenings, when household chores have exhausted their hold on the 'me' who appears to be writing this text, and the couch and big screen extend their invitation, 'I' will watch more than one movie at a sitting. Last night the last half of the Ralph Fiennes recent updating of Shakespeare's *Coriolanus* merged somewhat with the opening of that early seventies classic *Chinatown*, both of which called up my recent memories (from the night before) of another update – a new version of Henry James's *What Maisie Knew.* So warriors from Ancient Rome toting machine guns around a trashed urban nightmare looking not unlike parts of Syria, melded with bickering and jousting parents of contemporary New York and the criminal/political underworld of 1930's Los Angeles. Ruminating on them all later, I could see my consciousness focusing on this character and that, watching their actions, feeling their fears, ambitions and hidden motivations, their Achilles' heels, their pride and vanities, their idealisms, their corruptible natures and ultimately their desire to be loved. For moments I could see and feel them all, major players and minor supports, undergoing their dramas, testing themselves in conflict and in love, pursuing power, advantage, and resolution, sometimes all at the same time.

Surely this was how Higher Self experienced her personalities struggling through their issues in time and space, focusing on one and then the other, processing many channels of information simultaneously, seeing harmonies and dissonances in action and motivation, seeing the evolutions of anxieties, ambitions, and attitudes. How the fears of one widow (20) poisons the insecurities of another young mother (11) and pushes another lost soul (10) on the verge of giving up ever closer to suicide while, at the same time, edging another, (19), so close to self-immolation that she somehow rebounded into feisty inflammation, shoving the father-in-law – who's about to rape her – backwards into a stone wall where he cracks his skull and collapses. She pays for her unforgivable infraction but her child is born free and clear, later assuming the reins of power she could never get close to. Of course (12) and (21), being too bemused and pleasured by their own gratifications, are barely affected. Doubt and despair hardly ever enter their reality tunnels and, when they do so, are experienced as not much more than the flickering shadows of a fire no longer needed.

The characters in the movies are not karmically related of course, but I can see their ambitions, anxieties, and actions intertwining, producing comparisons and contrasts in a similar manner. By thus indulging myself, I am accumulating a small data bank of human action and motivation, which not only adds to my own repertoire but also informs my understanding with many shades and subtleties that I might miss in my own petty dramas.

So, even when 'I' am not moving into any of the several levels of harmony possible with Higher Self, I can glimpse reflections of not only its style but also its substance. 'I' can feel the director of many movies moving within the 'me' that aspires to be him, even though 'I', in microcosm, already am. Perhaps it is all about expanding into the greater self that is already there, filling up the apparently empty spaces with the consciousness that you assumed was small and bounded by the limited experience of the short life you assumed was yours and yours only. Perhaps blowing yourself up like some balloon, stretching yourself thinner and thinner over great distances until you are an infinitesimal skein covering a cloud of knowing; perhaps ultimately, that's all it is.

In this I am immediately reminded of some remarks by Charles Leadbeater in his volume *The Inner Life (1910)*. In the interests of illumination and accuracy I shall quote directly from the book, the section being 'The Aura Of A Deva':

> The fluctuations in the aura of a deva are so great as to be startling to those who are not used to them. One who recently did us the honour

to pay us a visit at Adyar, to give us information about the foundation of the sixth root-race, had normally an aura of about one hundred and fifty yards in diameter; but when he became interested in the teaching which he was giving to us, that aura increased until it reached the sea, which is about one mile away from us.

23

INDIVIDUALS, ARCHETYPES, AND FANTASIES

S everal sources, some traditional, some contemporary, insist that there is no such thing as an individuality; that it is an illusion, a vanity treasured by that name cavorting through its incarnation, a temporary identity, tagged on entry but soon to be dissolved into the waves of time and space splashing on the shores of posterity. The vanity of ambition and pride has already been pointed out by (26) and Gordon, already familiar with the argument, found himself bemused by the insistence with which it was delivered, contrasting that dissolution into nirvana with (12)'s embrace of the divine mother role.

In seeing (12)'s contribution as somehow more valuable than (26), he knew he was favouring one aspect over another, even though each contribution could easily be ascertained in his own brew of elements and his current exploration of all possible interactions with consciousness and society. Are we all, then, illusions of the Monad, he wonders. *Feeling* real, he knows, is not sufficient. *Defining* real might be more useful.

Yes, he knows such an enterprise usually winds up in the false security of materialism. Hurting the toes when you kick the stone only reasserts the sensitivity of nerve endings. The body's apparatus disappears with death and, from the other side of that divide, its facility seems as dreamlike as any other attribute of the physical plane.

If each and every projection of Monad/Higher Self can be met and merged with, surely it must assume some level of independent volition? The exploring consciousness – in this case, 'Gordon' – experiences them as real as any human character he knows in his incarnational world. Their dramas are done, perhaps, but their evocation of them can be just as vigorous as any friend here describing a divorce, political opponent, or tragic demise of a loved one. Gordon knows they could well be acting for his benefit, like all actors anywhere do. And, of course, the notion that everyone is acting anyway is never far from his mind. Is it only their relative attachment to their act which defines them? Some play the game amusedly and merrily while others seem attached to the sacredness of their every move. Gordon imagines Monad gathering it all in regardless.

It has not escaped Gordon's attention that all these characters in his cast can be seen as archetypes as well as incarnations. As contributions to his psyche they could function just as well. The contemplative monk, the secretly pagan priest, the heretical philosopher, the courtesan, the grieving widow, the anxious young mother, the rich and carefree playgirl, the vain bisexual playboy, the ruthless warrior, the passionate freedom fighter, the scholar king, the orphaned peasant girl: each is an archetype of behaviour, a psychological case study which any class or course could be built around. Here he is seeing psychology as a limited form of incarnational studies, illuminating some of the mysteries of the psyche but not the complex interactions through time and space which produce the infinite subtleties, and shades of grey comprising the big picture. That's one of at least four dimensions, the fourth being time, that enigmatic trickster which allows the costume dramas to appear distinct and unique.

Nor has it escaped his attention that many could see these individuals as fantasies based on what Gordon lacks and/or his frustrated ambitions. The tempting glamour of fame and notoriety in a past life is well known in the new age community, never mind that seemingly endless collection of the closed-minds that we call sceptics. Knowing that even the most evidential of past-lives-recalled cases are criticised and debunked, Gordon cares not to enter that fray. He knows that each incarnate soul must traverse the length and breadth of its brain-induced doubts to arrive at its own inner knowing, and thus he prefers to illustrate rather than attempt to convince, if, indeed, it is he who is doing the illustration.

While he sees incarnations full of twists and turns and knows that readers will thusly tune in, he is not threatened that others may see interesting archetypes worthy of study; and yet others may see fantasies fit only for a comic book or Hollywood movie. He understands that there are many ways to the illumination that some may call the truth. He is comfortable with his.

24

THE MONAD, NOW

Gordon is seated in a coffee shop, watching snowflakes slant and skitter about, and, with his laptop at the ready, wonders if he might, without further ado or deep ritual of meditation, merge with Monad, bringing that consciousness into his incarnate moment.

At first he wonders where Monad is, then quickly realises it is, of course, nowhere and everywhere. Why then, if it is everywhere, why can it not be here with me now?

I am, it says. *Feel me.* He does, bit by bit uncovering the all-knowing/seeing being-ness at his core; that being who just is – thoughts, emotions, anxieties, and any number of dissonances passing through it like breezes. It exists untouched, unperturbed, and still as a lake surface on a windless dawn. Gordon looks at the collection of customers in the café and sees their unconscious connection to their Higher Selves/Monads, knowing that even as they check their screens, scratch their noses and sip their drinks, they are all exploratory extensions of eternal multidimensional beings who sent them here with original inspiration to be and to learn whatever they needed to learn, adding to their earlier skills, techniques, and applications peculiar to the modern world, so that, when this planet playground has run its course, Monads will have full complements of many-wounded and multi-talented souls with which to engage guidance activities elsewhere in the multiverse.

Gordon more or less knows all this, but is happy to have his knowing thusly refreshed.

While more mundane thoughts and perceptions make their presence felt, he runs his flag up the antahkarana to the Monadic plane to exist as a blip of light in a sea of light. It is a tenuous connection at best, but at least a tiny probe of his consciousness is there. 'His' Monad has arranged a display, or is arranging it now. He feels suspended at a distance, a distance from what, let's say a satellite farther from its planet than usual. Instead of the twinkling against the inky blackness of interstellar space, he sees what seems like giant shifting textures of light, pinkish, golden, creamy. Shapes like small planets, say moons, appear and hang there. To be observed, he thinks. Are they real, he wonders? *Everything is real*, he hears, *even the unreal and the illusory. Real to the perceiver.*

Well, that's that one answered, he thinks. As the small planets weave in and around each other, like a ballet in space, one of them seems to have some kind of portal, not unlike those stairs on wheels that are brought to landed planes for disembarking, which unfolds out of a smooth pristine surface and from which roll out dozens of tiny replica planets, bluish in colour, contrasting nicely with their pinkish source and, as they join the intricate interplay, Gordon seems to see them abundant with life, that is lively activity of sentient forms. He kind of zooms in on them and sees strange but somehow recognisable creatures in alien-seeming landscapes and communities and zooms back out to see the small baby blue spheres swaying about prettily in and around the larger pinkish spheres.

Then the smaller bluish spheres morph into humanoid figures somehow large enough to be discerned and, as they sway to and fro in the mysterious choreography, Gordon once again seems able to zoom in and merge with one after another of these humanoid figures. Each one has a complete complement of attitudes and beliefs about themselves and their world's, life plans, strategies, accomplishments and regrets, all of which seem to be of a piece and impossible to discredit, real as real can be, so indisputably human that Gordon can only empathise. One after another each of these cosmic beings appears to be made up of a multitude of human frailties; wounds which characterise their strengths. *The scars of wisdom* is the phrase which Gordon feels inserted in his consciousness.

Then, after this zooming in and out, the giant seeming humanoid figures morph back into the smaller sized blue spheres and file back into the larger pinkish sphere they emerged from, seconds or centuries before, and the staircase/portal closes up neatly behind them. It is all so cartoon-like; even more so when the larger pinkish spheres merge into the slightly rose-hued slightly golden-textured background and he is left somehow alone to contemplate his elaborate fantasy. An inner voice tells him to *come back again sometime* and *see Act Two* for himself. Which, in the 'later' of this world of ours, he does. This time he is presented with an urban streetscape, busy with cars and pedestrians. Midday, everything is going smoothly. He seems to be simultaneously above and beside the action. Two places at once or no place at all? He decides to stop wondering and just watch. Everyone seems to be on automatic pilot, going about their business. He recalls, as a younger man, feeling that folk just weren't paying attention. Now he sees that the 'automatic pilot' perception is to indicate how much of their consciousness is elsewhere, that much of the soul energy is preoccupied with activities on planes other than the physical. A man of middle age and portly frame, perhaps an accountant or a lawyer at lunch, is somehow brought to his attention. Gordon finds his perception following a string of golden light leading away from his crown chakra up through the blue sky and into another dimension, where it leads to a family gathering, a happy picnic in either a large garden or a small park, where people are seated comfortably, sipping, nibbling, and chatting.

Of course, these are dead people, family members who have passed, enjoying their paradise in the knowledge that others will join them sooner or later. The man appears more or less like himself as he crosses the street; perhaps a little less preoccupied and more chatty as he raises his glass and grins. Gordon sees the line of golden light leading away from his crown once again and finds himself, or his perceptions, following it to another sphere or dimension; he's not sure, but it is a gathering space in some spirit world city and he sees the man, now younger and more radiant, in a group listening to a speaker. A teacher, an inspirer. This is the man's future, his afterlife existence. The same golden thread leads him to some type of temple, elegant and inspiring, in which the man sits crossed-legged, meditating in a group of like-minded others. A glimpse of this and then he's gone and Gordon sees him flying to one of the pinkish globes from before.

Then he's back at the midday street scene. A mother with a child in a stroller is in focus. Golden streams from both their heads entwine, leading his vision upward and away. He sees the woman seated with two men and knows that one is her husband and the other the baby to be. Heads are bowed and discussion seems serious. Then he sees the woman and husband coupling and an orb hovering above. Then he sees the couple and the child travelling in a car suddenly crushed by falling rocks on a mountainside pass. Then the three of them in some kind of astral resort surfing the waves in their bare feet with uncanny precision. Then the three of them as ethereal transparencies twirling about each other daintily. Then the three of them flying towards another pinkish globe.

Then he's back at the midday street scene, relaxed and observant as though nothing out of the ordinary had occurred. An elderly man moves slowly along the sidewalk. The golden thread leading from his crown chakra entices Gordon into what seems like a past life as a dropped-behind-enemy-lines commando, who parachutes into a field by a forest, buries his parachute and walks into the forest. A small town later he has lodgings, street clothes, and two suitcases, one of which has a sniper's rifle. He sees him on a train to a bigger city where he is given a room high above a street. When a parade goes by he shoots a general waving to the crowds. When he is caught escaping, a small revolver in his pocket cuts short his captor's urge for torture. Gordon sees his spirit hovering over the chaotic scene and then follows it to a heaven world in which the man obviously believes. A greeting party congratulates and celebrations ensue. The vibrational effects of the war obviously continue here. He sees him in a country cottage gardening. Then a visit back to Earth. A humble home with a young family: his daughter, her husband and a young child. Then the woman is pregnant and the war hero hovers as an orb and then settles in the womb. Then Gordon is back at the street scene watching the elderly man lean on a lamppost and struggle for breath. Passers-by come to his aid and he faints into their arms.

Gordon sees the spirit exit and hover as panic ensues. He watches the spirit watching. He sees a guide lead it away and follows discreetly to the spirit world reception centre. Then, it's a reuniting with the wife from the war years, who'd always kinda wondered about her grandson, and had her suspicions confirmed when arriving back in spirit herself. Gordon sees them settle in much the same – if not exactly the same – cottage the man had gardened in before. Domestic bliss in eternity.

Doubtless these two will live out their heaven lives and remerge with their Monad, masquerading as a pinkish sphere, but Gordon doesn't see that. Not this time anyway.

He returns to normal consciousness; ponders on the marvellously adaptable process which enables such learning curves to unfold in time and space. Then he chuckles, seeing how it must be all in a day's work for Monad. Or maybe a moment's unfolding. An inner voice, that inner voice, says *Is that enough for now?* Gordon believes it is. But is that just another belief system that tempts him with its parameters? And the Monad itself, swimming in its sea of divinity, is that a belief system poised to impose its version of sentience? Gordon would prefer to transcend these questions, however titillating to the intellect they might be. Though Monad is the All in the Now, surely, like all created beings in the multiverse, it must have an evolutionary arc matched to its potential? Gordon rather fancies that to be the case, but suspects he will have to resort to the channellings of Alice Bailey for a fuller understanding.

25

HOW ALL THIS MAKES ME FEEL

As one emerges into this mysterious atmosphere where the Monad seems to have its being and opens oneself to the seeming omnipresence and relative omniscience of its existence, one feels smaller and smaller until 'what I did in this incarnation' becomes little more than 'what I did today', the major events and life changers assuming the more humble mantle of, say, a bashed thumb, a sad memory, or after-dinner indigestion. All that excitement, anxiety, and unpleasant drama just dribbles away into details – some annoying, some as yet alluring.

As I examine these details, once so intensely important, I can see just how they might become mere files in the data banks of Higher Self/Monad. Firstly I get more and more distanced from their dramatics, experiencing them in my astral body as emotional residues, then in my mental body as inflamed thoughts, and then in my causal body as driving forces of an incarnation, and then in my buddhic body as flashes of character-building inspiration, quickly conceived and even more quickly forgotten, and then, in joys and pleasures of Paradise they melt into the deep background of the life as lived and then into the deep background of all human lives, the curses and blessings which promote all change and growth.

When I no longer care one way or the other, I can, as we say, let it all go, and from there to files in the data banks of Higher Self which is an effortless switch. All passion spent, all promise fulfilled, all causes catered to. And in the process many lives become one. The deep throb of the rock, the dry itch and damp sponge of the soil, the electric thrill of sunlight on plant, the cool glide of the fish, the sharp joy of flight, the dead weight of gravity, the pangs of all hungers, the bonds of all loves.

How it makes me feel: a servant who sees the master in himself, a detail who knows the full design, a hobbit who no longer craves the ring, a willing harmony to a beautiful song, a pawn who dines with bishop and king, a partisan who knows the heart of his oppressor, a messenger who's swallowed the message.

And who, you might ask, is me? Any definition will do for now.

26

BEMUSED AFTERWORD

At the end of *More Adventures In Eternity* (2008), I appended a list of ten Eternal Life Tips, designed to amuse the ambitious but now perhaps befuddled reader. Number ten was: *The parts you played before, and the parts you will play, can, and often do, influence you in the moment. If the subconscious drives and motivations of conventional psychology seem daunting, wait till you get a handle on this.*

And it can be rather crazy-making, as if every supporting part in Hamlet was protruding into our hero's thoughts and polluting his speeches. I have attempted to illustrate the way around that; yet in doing so I have neglected one soul probe whose influence is more than pervasive for the Gordon who has been narrating. (9), a young girl who passed in an automobile accident over a century ago, has seemed, over the years of Gordon's span, to be somehow in residence in his psyche. Not a possession or obsession as the current literature details, but more of an invited guest. Her contribution to his anima is profound. There have been times when his masculinity was not only balanced by her but almost overwhelmed, and yet at no point did he feel the urge for a sex change as described in the memoirs of those who have dared the leap. His gender identification was solid.

At one point in his trek across modern times Gordon came to see that this inner girl, this innocent maid growing up within him, was the source for not only many of his projections of female grace and charm on the women around him, but also his shyness and sensitivity in the rituals of courtship. Many years later, when (9), through Gordon's contacts and interpersonal frictions, had matured, the more knowledgeable and confident influences of (12), (21) and (17) held sway, with occasional destabilising irruptions from (10), (19) and (20), bringing their anguish and anxiety into play. Is she yet resident, Gordon wonders from time to time? The answer seems to be: they have merged, quite completely, with androgyny being the outcome.

(9)'s early passing seemed very much like a set-up for the learning curve of her then parents, both of whom Gordon knows in his current life, but, interestingly, have had no contact with each other, nor are likely to. Gordon's perception of the girl's relief at passing, obtained during a regression, seemed equalled only by her almost complete lack of attachment to the troubled family life she'd so recently quit. Gordon only wished that he could so easily detach from the many dramas of his day.

In this life, where each of the parents has retained their earlier gender, Gordon, as he passed through their lives, felt a deep and mysteriously comparable love for both and, when in intimate contact with the woman, often felt like one flesh, obviously an echo from 'before'. Interestingly neither could accept his tale of past life connections, which was also the case with the re-experienced drama of (8), whose suicide left a wife and family uprooted, and whose present day replica Gordon would have loved to make up to in some way, had she been in any way open to the possibility, which she most definitely was not. Gordon has learned to accept that what is a welcome revelation for him may not be for the others with whom such psychic entanglement has become a way of life, albeit unconscious. Many, as we know, find one life to be more than enough for now, thank you.

And when you've linked up all the seemingly disparate lives in the chain, all the lost chapters in the book, the many lives become one anyway. No wonder I'm bemused.

27

APPENDIX ONE: HENRY REAPPEARS

Henry, Gordon's enigmatic teacher and guide during the emergence of the out-of-body experiences, which resulted in the first book of this trilogy, *Eternal Life And How To Enjoy It* and in some of its successor, *More Adventures In Eternity*, has been requisitioned to appear here to satisfy the many requests from readers over the years.

When he chooses to be in human form in those flexible realities of spirit where he is currently focused, he plays the part of a caretaker gardener in a delightfully sprawling estate that is used by those in recovery from various afflictions of the brain and nervous system; afflictions whose residue yet resonates in their afterlife realities.

Much has been quietly contrived to ease the tensions of the estate's many visitors and wanderers. Even the wildlife has been especially invited. Many of the visitors stay in a series of rest homes ringing the estate at irregular intervals. Henry just kind of wanders about absentmindedly with a small wheelbarrow of tools in tow, and stops to chat and joke.

As you can no doubt imagine he's a caretaker of souls as much as anything else and he wants you to know he enjoys his current position as much as anything he has tried. Come here when you can, he invites, and I'll make sure to hide. Are you part of Gordon's Monad, and are you two connected in past lives, 'I' ask, repeating the questions often pitched to 'me'? He flashes a grin and disappears. I try to disappear after him, the anarchic rascal, but invisibility cloaks us both and I 'see' I've been had. Again.

28

APPENDIX TWO: ESSAYS FROM THE ONLINE BLOG

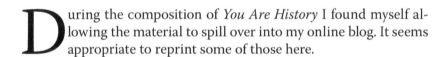

During the composition of *You Are History* I found myself allowing the material to spill over into my online blog. It seems appropriate to reprint some of those here.

Teaching Access to the God Consciousness

Teaching access to the God consciousness is not my only path as a facilitator, but it is one I feel especially cut out for. Something that, in the early days of my awakening, in this incarnation, I grew to be quite passionate about. It felt to me, particularly after the writing of my second book, *More Adventures in Eternity*, that it was a major life task; one that "I" had held over, in abeyance, since Ancient Egypt, when I learned the hard way, in the struggles of competing priesthoods, that many stood to lose status and career if such a path was laid open to the masses.

I learned, mainly through guides in the afterlife 'phase' of that Egyptian priest incarnation, that such an impassioned vocation, was ultimately out of place in that highly evolved yet spiritually restrained culture. Only a few were actually ready for such radical innovation. The divine will of the mass expressed itself, ultimately, much as voters do in elections, in favour of, deference to, and dependence on, priesthoods. Priesthoods as revered elites of functioning intermediaries. Elites with specialised access to the divine.

But for a short interlude in ancient Britain, where as a Druid priest "I" understood and imparted such esoteric teachings to students, the last two thousand odd years have been spent in the shadows of such teachings, while the dark ages of organised religion, with its ruthless repression of anything even resembling dissent, held sway.

Now, in this new millennium, we have, at least some of us, the freedom to pursue spiritual exploration, both as teachers and students. And what a joy it is, to observe a roomful of seminar attendees as their consciousness, under guidance, moves out through the crown chakra, up the antahkarana, through the many planes of spirit, the many spheres of post-mortem and out of body activity, and on through the formless energy planes to the Monadic level, where they reunite with their Higher Selves (source self/group soul/Monad) and experience some measure of that seemingly omniscient and omnipresent consciousness that is a very near neighbour to the God consciousness. There, they can, depending on their willingness to open up and expose their limited personal consciousness, have a taste of the eternal now endlessly recreating itself, endlessly exfoliating more and more forms, the proverbial ten thousand things emerging and returning to the One every nanosecond.

Amongst other things, I might add. Being, say, many 'past' incarnations, ...human, 'alien', animal, bird, fish, river, tree, cloud, and so on. The worlds of the huge (planets, galaxies) to the worlds of the tiny (sub-atomic particles).

When they return to the bodies and normal consciousness, knowing that each will have experienced their own unique level of exposure, I encourage them to take notes quickly, before the exalted expansion dissipates entirely. Then we share and discuss.

What I have discovered over these recent years is that while there is a steady but small supply of students who wish to thus extend their consciousness, there is a larger group who want to (a) connect with their spirit guides, (b) contact their deceased loved ones, (c) learn energy healing, chakra balancing, Reiki and the other popular psychic abilities. And how, you might ask, do I feel about this?

Well, like many other issues in life, my reaction depends upon my ever changing moods. So with that in mind I would question any answer that catapults one reaction into the spotlight and leaves the others languishing in the shadows. That I react at all is a given, of course, but I have learned to take it all in stride and not favour one client's stated needs over another. It's all spiritual growth of one kind or another. It's all expansion of consciousness, however temporary. It's all revelation, maybe amusingly mild, maybe belief system shaking.

You can talk to annoying ghosts, deceased loved ones, fairies, angels, aliens, archangels, prophets, saints and ascended masters. You can access and transmit energy healing, you can divine with crystals and pendulums, you can telepath with animals, feel cancerous tumours as living beings exercising their free will. You can exit your body and fly about. You can access and understand your earlier journeys through various forms. You can embrace Gaia, or at least that portion that will fit into your grasp.

But you can also merge with the God consciousness and know, however briefly, its boundless energy and endless creativity, its transcendence of form, emotion, and thought. Why evolution is merely the play of Maya, the Goddess amusing herself with the chattering and crying of her children. Why planets are useful playgrounds and religions good shepherds gone bad. Why the sheep are content to graze and reproduce while the enlightened look on bemused. Why you are one of the sheep *and* one of the enlightened.

The Ancient Wisdom and Society

As we progress with this work and deepen our understanding of the subtleties and complexities of our incarnational journeys towards graduation we uncover more and more of ourselves at the important junctures and transitions that we once assumed were administered by remote angelic entities and divinities.

We discover that there isn't just the *you* on trial for your shortcomings as you slowly pay off your earthly debts, but another *you* who flies about giddy with pleasure and excitement every night during sleep and sometimes visits the loved ones you grieve during the daylight hours. And there are other *yous* living in different epochs and societies, struggling with their problems and making their contributions. And yet another *you* who never left home, not for one microsecond, so comfortable is she with the bliss of omniscience and omnipresence, preferring to dispatch a series of explorers into the realms of density and darkness.

Lately we've been accommodating ourselves to the notion that one of these *yous* makes many of the major life choices before entering the drama down here. We're coming to understand that much of the challenge, anguish, and danger we wade through is carefully selected to expose us in ways we either have never faced before, or did face but, as we say, kinda flunked.

Of course, many devoted religionists will say that this *you* of whom we speak is actually God, whereas we feel it is that part of us closest to divinity. While I don't see that disparity changing anytime soon, it does speak of a certain similarity of outlook which quietly belies our oh-so-apparent differences.

I was pondering these issues as I watched a recent BBC drama, *"Exile"* with Jim Broadbent & John Simm, where, as a final act of anger and disgust, the protagonist spat into the open grave of the man who had forcefully abused his unknown mother, causing his conception and later adoption. This act was the culmination of much personal investigative work into a sex abuse scandal at a local mental institution many years before.

Whilst the drama was consistently well scripted, acted, and dramatically convincing, I couldn't help but wonder how that man might have reacted had he known of all the research into the between-life state that has given us so much more understanding of the wide variety of life choices available to the incoming soul. That research, expanding dramatically these past few years, has led us to feel that very little of consequence is left to the old paradigm called *chance*. While there are many questions left to be answered, the picture being built is one of careful planning and choice predicated on past failures and fresh challenges.

Various qualities need to be developed at every stage of the unfolding, sometimes it's courage, sometimes restraint, sometimes giddy emotional indulgence and others strict adherence to rules and regulations. When souls are young, inexperienced and headstrong, obedience to established authority is required but, later, when those same souls are mature and responsibly creative, traditional authorities need to be ignored. And, when authorities are corrupt, they need to be overthrown. As tribes struggle and coalesce into nations, various qualities need to be developed and then released. There are no hard and fast rules for all creation, other than maybe constant change. Free-thinking flexibility seems to be the guideline that comes up over and over again. What was wise and maybe sacred in one epoch may be foolish and short-sighted in another.

Again, whilst the majority of incoming souls at this advanced stage of Gaia's growth take 'time' to plan their course work, and fit into a family and nation suitable to their needs and challenges, there are some young hotheads who rush back into incarnation, eschewing advice and warnings, so desperate are they for the thrill of physicality. Souls like that can, and do, end up in the wombs of poor unfortunates with little chance of any kind of life enhancement. Often because that's all that's left after the good pickings are gone.

Obviously, while some careful souls will actually choose an awful situation to be born into, just for the challenge of struggling upward and out, most of us have advanced beyond such. When I say "most of us" I am, of course, speaking to that amorphous group of mature and older souls who have helped map the territory by participating in regression work over the decades. As young souls tend not to be interested in such arcane activities, we have but the little information uncovered by those who would go back far enough to their days as a young soul and report on their hasty choices and afterlife remorse and huffiness (Charles Breaux's *The Way Of Karma* is particularly good in this regard). And, as such, we are forced to extrapolate from the patterns so far uncovered.

Will the appalling and tawdry dramas, like the one mentioned above, continue as long as there are souls willing to undergo such trials to cobble together a character out of such grim raw materials? Unlike the sunnier of new-age voices who predict the ascension process will wither such situations, I tend to think so. When we look to the countries tearing themselves apart in vicious civil wars around the globe we have to assume only young souls careless of weighty karma would supply themselves so unwittingly. When I turn my inner eye to some of these countries I see souls rapidly returning from vicious deaths to child soldierdom in appalling numbers, with tribal affiliations as the unbreakable bond and hypnotising glue.

When you read in old esoteric texts of the powerful hold "folk-souls" can have on their folk, as I have in my formative years, look to these trouble spots around the globe where the individual essence is repeatedly sacrificed on the altar of tribal Gods and demented notions of religious purity. To provide a reference point, let me mention the British folksoul, of which I am more familiar. It expresses itself more these days in sports such as soccer, as opposed to the days of 1914 when millions mindlessly flocked to the seemingly pointless slaughter. As such, it is typical of many of the European folksouls, now resigned to a lesser role, while those of South American countries are currently in the ascendant.

As I communicate with other explorers and researchers in this field, we're cheered by how much has been uncovered in this last century, particularly the last fifty years, but we are under no illusions as to how much there is yet to be revealed. And, as such, further revelations may render my above speculations close to redundant. Certainly our understanding of the reincarnation cycle, in its now seemingly infinite variety of patterns, has deepened greatly over what was considered cutting edge as recently as 1980, when the notion of planning your incarnation, without the controlling oversight of folk like *The Lords Of Karma*, so beloved by the early Theosophists, was fresh and new.

What's cutting edge now? Well, for my money, it's much as I indicated in *More Adventures In Eternity*: the understanding that from Higher Self – which we truly and indisputably are, if only in microcosm – all incarnations, with their sufferings and joys and learning, are happening simultaneously, and that somehow, the progression we feel as "souls getting smarter", is an illusion evolving out of the dramas of history, so predictably linear to our normal mode of perception, and that somehow Higher Self is already enlightened from experience on other planetary systems and yet is willing to give that up temporarily to undergo the specific educational path designed for Gaia and her team.

Certainly when I identify with "Gordon" and look at the past lives I feel I've uncovered so far, I do feel like, if not the wisest, then one of the wisest. But when I merge with Higher Self, that intelligence tells me that in each "tryout for the team" I decided beforehand how much soul wisdom I would bring with me, the 30%, 50% or 70% referred to by other between-life researchers, so that whatever amount I manifested in any "tryout" was not what was actually available, but merely what was "borrowed" from the reserves in Higher Self.

Whether others, or many others, will corroborate this insight in the years to come, remains a great fascination for me. That is, this *me* writing this.

Defending Your Country
Here in the Toronto area we are currently undergoing the media frenzy around TIFF, the Toronto International Film Festival. Every day you can hear interviews, reviews and comments on the state of film and society, most of them engaging.

A couple of days ago I came in on the middle of an interview and a female voice was saying how she just *had* to defend her country, and that no other option was available to her. If I'm not mistaken it was a section of a documentary on Syria by a Canadian director, the name of which now escapes me. But it was the sentiment and the power with which it was expressed which caught me.

This was a soul determined to sacrifice whatever personal goals had matured within her for the passionate commitment to her soil and forefathers. While to many of us in the 'free west' such single minded determination may seem short sighted and foolish, we are products of many past lives, some of which were diverted by tribal and nationalist causes. We, it would seem, have internalised the lessons of the 'patriot's game'.

Souls, caught up in civil wars, incarnated with that possibility front and centre in their agenda, along with whatever personal and family karma they wished to pursue. Of course, they may not recall much of that 'now', not any more than you or I in the course of our daily tasks and games. But while we worry over the actions of our governments in these seemingly intractable problems – where every idealistic assertion is shrouded in self-serving propaganda and worse, lies – let us recall that we, as souls slightly lower on the spiral of evolutionary tendencies, once felt such passions deeply. I know 'I' did.

There's at least one 'freedom fighter' in my soul history, and his energetic presence is often perceptible to the current projection known as Gordon. Although he lived in the 13th century and participated in an ongoing guerrilla war against a mighty oppressor, his attitudes, habits, and moral fervour are a regular part of my 'make-up'. Of course, other 'past lives' have their resonance within 'me', but this fellow is prominent 'now'. I feel his passion and determination and transmute it from the temptations of anger, outrage and righteousness into something more civil and courtly like, intellectual polemic, cafe-centered debate and carefree 'jokeyness'. The effort sometimes lapses, of course, and the surly, self-righteous grouch gets to have his way for a moment or two. Or three.

Did that soul reach his pinnacle of fulfilment? Yes, I believe he did, although the struggle to rid Scotland of its oppressors continued into the next phase of uniting the religions and tribes into what became, eventually, Great Britain. That success, of course, slid inexorably into the British Empire, powered, as some of you may know, by reincarnating Roman souls who wished to 'get it right this time', and then by returning Greeks, who thought 'let's add some decent culture and democratic principles to this giant multinational mercantile enterprise'. Needless to say, those souls in my 'soul family' who actively participated in this centuries-long process also have their energetic influence upon the 'me' who deliberates upon and writes this.

But it's the freedom fighter, excoriating his men for laxity and gobbling down his much needed meals while he has the chance, who was roused by this Syrian woman declaring her passionate destiny.

29

APPENDIX THREE

Ruminating on what might have been missed in the main sur-
vey of *You Are History*, it occurred to '*me*' that there were some
gaps in conveying how 'Gordon' sees, or does not quite see, the
position his future selves may, or may not, occupy. Right from 2004,
when Cassiopeia intruded on the text of *More Adventures in Eternity*,
Gordon had puzzled over the implied paradox of his supposed free will
and the already established existence of a future self. Not a probable
self, but an incarnation already in progress. The intellectual ferment
of that puzzle faded with the busy details of 'time' but never completely disappeared. Until now, that is. A few days ago Higher Self kindly
stepped in and straightened out the wrinkles. Oh joy!

"I see my probe Gordon admiring his future self Cassiopeia and
wondering how on Earth he'll ever get there through the trudges
of time and temptations of Paradise, not to mention the bliss of
non-being, and I feel what humans would think of as and chuckle.
The process will be as easy as putting on a new pair of shoes but
Gordon will have to fight against his resistance, some of which is
the embarrassing ghost of predestination, that ugly remnant of Prot-
estant theology which chained its adherents to lives with no possibility of change, and some is its modern mirror image, free will,
which insists that souls can do anything they want at any juncture,
which is, in its own way true.

Gordon wonders what might occur if he chooses not to incarnate as Cassiopeia; would that relegate her to some sci-fi parallel universe of dreamy possibility, but not actual life with shared characteristics and karma. He could so choose, but Cassiopeia can be fashioned out of the soul energies of other so-called earlier probes from this here Monad, many of whom share the necessary ingredients for her exposition of the ongoing experiment. Cassiopeia will come into being whether 'Gordon' contributes or not, and I know he understands already that what he has to contribute, should he choose to do so, is not exactly 'his'. It's 'mine', although he is 'me' and I am 'him', and as he thinks, smiling, of John Lennon's "And we are all together" I see Cassiopeia joyfully expressing the mid-air balletics she is so good at to her young pupils, and feeling, in her own way, the thoughts we are sharing.

She sees Gordon as clearly as he sees several of his 'pasts' – the Druid, the courtesan, the king, the philosopher, and so on – even more clearly perhaps, given her higher vibration, more explicit evolution and greater acceptance of how *'she'* fits into *'me'*. Gordon tells me he feels strangely liberated when he hears of this. He then tells me it's something like having your cake and eating it too.

30

APPENDIX FOUR

During the winter of 1998/99, when I was committing the then strange and wonderful experiences 'Gordon' was having, whilst asleep, to paper, the ones that would become the first part of this trilogy, *Eternal Life And How To Enjoy It*, my guide through the afterlife realms, Henry, conducted me to a 'place' where I could view some of my past lives. After expressing his concern at containing my excitement at the prospect, he said the reward would be "an understanding of how all his lives are indissolubly linked, not only to each other but also to the evolution of the planet itself and all the life-forms on it."

His impression as to the organising of the display was given to Higher Self, one "of those lovely translucent onions…dwelling on that level which is the first energy step down from the God level" and who thus have "almost unlimited powers". I recalled the visuals of the experience as "about twenty large television sets suspended in front of you in two tiers. You press a button and all the screens come to life".

"Starting on the bottom left he sees a baby swathed in animal skins, sleeping by an open fire in what could be a cave…no one else seems to be around. To the right is an image of a middle aged man, again dressed in animal skins. Standing in a river he appears to be spearing fish." Then we see "Two brothers building a house from large rocks" in a "virtually treeless land". Next screen displays "a domestic dispute" with a "rough hewn table around which two men frown and gesture".

Tuning into the dialogue we hear that "slavery is the issue". As "small children cower in a corner, a brawl begins but is ended by a woman waving a shotgun". The ensuing struggle "triggers the death of one of the children" and a glance at other screens reveal (a) the lone baby eaten by wolves, (b) the happy fisherman, surrounded by sleeping children and engaged in merry intercourse with his wife, and (c) the two brothers on their deathbeds, sharing some disease."

Next there's a freeze frame of a "nun bent in prayer, a nurse attending to wounded soldiers by lamplight, a pretty girl raped behind a darkened building who then strikes her assailant with a hidden blade. Then an aristocratic lady entertaining her lover in her boudoir, where, like a cheap farce the husband enters on cue and, as he stabs the naked lover, we see he is also the rapist from the previous screen. We return to the nurse who lies abed praying for peace. The nun appears withdrawn in silent meditation in her darkened cell, a haven from all activity."

"Another woman, in some half-collapsed shack, dies in agonising childbirth, her two other children looking on appalled. We see the living with what appears to be an aunt, slaving at her whim. As teenagers they escape her cruelty, only to die in some plague. Screen right we see a happy couple, weavers by the look of it, adjourning from their work for a simple supper with two chattering children." The connections seemed obvious.

Then, in an intriguing hint of things to come: - "In order to simulate the all-at-once nature of these incarnations, the screens display the narratives in rapid-fire mode. There's a well-dressed boy lying by a brook in the long grass, obviously daydreaming. There's a woman at her wedding, the crowd solid and self-satisfied in a middle-class merchant sort of way. We see her later, slightly pregnant, taking lessons on the harpsichord. Another woman, her hair and manner wild, paints small canvases in what looks like a drafty attic with a dirty skylight. Another shelves books in a large library. Another, either born into or cast into poverty, gives herself to strangers in darkened alleys for pennies. The self-hatred is stunning."

"Back on the bottom row there's a couple of warriors, one at the peak of his physique, trouncing his enemies without any trouble, the other young and headstrong, an arrow in the heart at twenty."

"Next to these a couple of sedentary intellectuals. The first some kind of minister studying a bible, the second more like a philosopher debating with his gentlemen friends at dinner. We see the man of God defending himself in some ecclesiastical court and failing. Whatever the issues are, they're important to him and he returns home completely disaffected with his church. The philosopher dies old and contented, blessing all who surround him with his innate goodwill."

"On the female line there appear two scenes of women in distress. One sits in a castle bedroom, all stone walls and thick drapes, very pregnant and very lonely. Another stands on the seashore, shawl drawn about her shoulders, pining toward the horizon. One is wealthy, the other poor, but both are learning that loneliness knows no class bounds. One has only a demanding father-in-law, who thinks a weekly rape is his due and her solace, the other no father figure at all, only old women in time of war. Both turn to their young sons for sustenance, starting lifelong obsessions that stunt everyone's growth."

Although not all the above scenarios are included in my 'cast of characters' for *You Are History*, a surprising number are. I say surprising because during the composition of this work I never consulted *Eternal Life* for references, although portions of *More Adventures* were checked and quoted from. Why some past lives seem closer to Gordon than others is the usual 'mystery wrapped in an enigma' that keeps most folk at a safe distance from abstruse metaphysical speculations. Does he belong to a thread of lives that help make up the weave? Does Henry belong there too? Or not? Do the two feuding brothers from the American Civil War belong to another thread which Gordon can be aware of but not actually a living part? At least since the early 1930's – when Geraldine Cummins' channellings of Frederick Myers got the Spiritualist ball rolling on 'group souls', tying it irrevocably to earlier Theosophical texts on Monads – experiencers and researchers have puzzled over these apparent paradoxes, and I'm once again bemused to say that the shifting textures of the mystery remain tantalisingly shifting.

And as the unending torrent of words that is the writer's life continues to swamp the author that is currently '*me*', I suspect I'd mostly forgotten that a past life review sequence was included in the opening of the trilogy. I include it here for your bemused delectation. Is that a grin I see emerging? Or maybe a smirk?

BIBLIOGRAPHY

C. W. Leadbeater, *The Monad* (Theosophical Publishing House 1920)

C.W. Leadbeater, *The Inner Life* (Theosophical Publishing House 1978)

Annie Besant, *The Ancient Wisdom* (Theosophical Publishing House 1897)

Gregory J. Riley, *The River Of God* (Harper Collins 2001)

John Holman, *The Return Of The Perennial Philosophy* (Watkins 2008)

Gottfried de Purucker, *Fundamentals Of The Esoteric Philosophy* (Theosophical Uni. Press 1979)

Alice Bailey, *Initiation, Human and Solar* (Lucis Publishing 1922)

Alice Bailey, *Discipleship In The New Age* (Lucis Publishing 1955)

Alice Bailey, *A Treatise On Cosmic Fire* (Lucis Publishing 1925)

Christopher M. Bache, *Lifecycles* (Paragon House 1990)

Cyril Scott, *An Outline Of Modern Occultism* (Routledge and Kegan Paul 1950)

Jay Kinney ed., *The Inner West* (Tarcher/Penguin 2004)

Helena Blavatsky, *The Secret Doctrine* (The Theosophy Company 1974)

Ian Lawton, *Supersoul* (Rational Spirituality Press 2013)

Ian Lawton, *The Wisdom Of The Soul* (Rational Spirituality Press 2007)

Bruce Moen, The *Exploring The Afterlife* Series (Vols1-4 Hampton Roads 2001)

Jane Roberts, *Adventures In Consciousness* (Prentice Hall 1975)

Gordon Phinn, *Eternal Life And How To Enjoy It* (Hampton Roads 2004)

Gordon Phinn, *More Adventures In Eternity* (o-books 2008)

Gordon Phinn, *An American In Heaven* (o-books 2009)

Paperbacks also available from
White Crow Books

Elsa Barker—*Letters from
a Living Dead Man*
ISBN 978-1-907355-83-7

Elsa Barker—*War Letters from
the Living Dead Man*
ISBN 978-1-907355-85-1

Elsa Barker—*Last Letters from
the Living Dead Man*
ISBN 978-1-907355-87-5

Richard Maurice Bucke—
Cosmic Consciousness
ISBN 978-1-907355-10-3

Arthur Conan Doyle—
The Edge of the Unknown
ISBN 978-1-907355-14-1

Arthur Conan Doyle—
The New Revelation
ISBN 978-1-907355-12-7

Arthur Conan Doyle—
The Vital Message
ISBN 978-1-907355-13-4

Arthur Conan Doyle with
Simon Parke—*Conversations
with Arthur Conan Doyle*
ISBN 978-1-907355-80-6

Meister Eckhart with Simon Parke—
Conversations with Meister Eckhart
ISBN 978-1-907355-18-9

D. D. Home—*Incidents in my Life Part 1*
ISBN 978-1-907355-15-8

Mme. Dunglas Home; edited,
with an Introduction, by Sir
Arthur Conan Doyle—*D. D.
Home: His Life and Mission*
ISBN 978-1-907355-16-5

Edward C. Randall—
Frontiers of the Afterlife
ISBN 978-1-907355-30-1

Rebecca Ruter Springer—
Intra Muros: My Dream of Heaven
ISBN 978-1-907355-11-0

Leo Tolstoy, edited by Simon
Parke—*Forbidden Words*
ISBN 978-1-907355-00-4

Leo Tolstoy—*A Confession*
ISBN 978-1-907355-24-0

Leo Tolstoy—*The Gospel in Brief*
ISBN 978-1-907355-22-6

Leo Tolstoy—*The Kingdom
of God is Within You*
ISBN 978-1-907355-27-1

Leo Tolstoy—*My Religion:
What I Believe*
ISBN 978-1-907355-23-3

Leo Tolstoy—*On Life*
ISBN 978-1-907355-91-2

Leo Tolstoy—*Twenty-three Tales*
ISBN 978-1-907355-29-5

Leo Tolstoy—*What is Religion
and other writings*
ISBN 978-1-907355-28-8

Leo Tolstoy—*Work While
Ye Have the Light*
ISBN 978-1-907355-26-4

Leo Tolstoy—*The Death of Ivan Ilyich*
ISBN 978-1-907661-10-5

Leo Tolstoy—*Resurrection*
ISBN 978-1-907661-09-9

Leo Tolstoy with Simon Parke—
Conversations with Tolstoy
ISBN 978-1-907355-25-7

Howard Williams with an Introduction
by Leo Tolstoy—*The Ethics of Diet:
An Anthology of Vegetarian Thought*
ISBN 978-1-907355-21-9

Vincent Van Gogh with Simon Parke—
Conversations with Van Gogh
ISBN 978-1-907355-95-0

Wolfgang Amadeus Mozart with Simon
Parke—*Conversations with Mozart*
ISBN 978-1-907661-38-9

Jesus of Nazareth with Simon Parke—
Conversations with Jesus of Nazareth
ISBN 978-1-907661-41-9

Thomas à Kempis with Simon
Parke—*The Imitation of Christ*
ISBN 978-1-907661-58-7

Julian of Norwich with Simon
Parke—*Revelations of Divine Love*
ISBN 978-1-907661-88-4

Allan Kardec—*The Spirits Book*
ISBN 978-1-907355-98-1

Allan Kardec—*The Book on Mediums*
ISBN 978-1-907661-75-4

Emanuel Swedenborg—*Heaven and Hell*
ISBN 978-1-907661-55-6

P.D. Ouspensky—*Tertium Organum:
The Third Canon of Thought*
ISBN 978-1-907661-47-1

Dwight Goddard—*A Buddhist Bible*
ISBN 978-1-907661-44-0

Michael Tymn—*The Afterlife Revealed*
ISBN 978-1-970661-90-7

Michael Tymn—*Transcending the
Titanic: Beyond Death's Door*
ISBN 978-1-908733-02-3

Guy L. Playfair—*If This Be Magic*
ISBN 978-1-907661-84-6

Guy L. Playfair—*The Flying Cow*
ISBN 978-1-907661-94-5

Guy L. Playfair —*This House is Haunted*
ISBN 978-1-907661-78-5

Carl Wickland, M.D.—
Thirty Years Among the Dead
ISBN 978-1-907661-72-3

John E. Mack—*Passport to the Cosmos*
ISBN 978-1-907661-81-5

Peter & Elizabeth Fenwick—
The Truth in the Light
ISBN 978-1-908733-08-5

Erlendur Haraldsson—
Modern Miracles
ISBN 978-1-908733-25-2

Erlendur Haraldsson—
At the Hour of Death
ISBN 978-1-908733-27-6

Erlendur Haraldsson—
The Departed Among the Living
ISBN 978-1-908733-29-0

Brian Inglis—*Science and Parascience*
ISBN 978-1-908733-18-4

Brian Inglis—*Natural and Supernatural:
A History of the Paranormal*
ISBN 978-1-908733-20-7

Ernest Holmes—*The Science of Mind*
ISBN 978-1-908733-10-8

Victor & Wendy Zammit —*A Lawyer
Presents the Evidence For the Afterlife*
ISBN 978-1-908733-22-1

Casper S. Yost—*Patience
Worth: A Psychic Mystery*
ISBN 978-1-908733-06-1

William Usborne Moore—
Glimpses of the Next State
ISBN 978-1-907661-01-3

William Usborne Moore—
The Voices
ISBN 978-1-908733-04-7

John W. White—
The Highest State of Consciousness
ISBN 978-1-908733-31-3

Stafford Betty—
The Imprisoned Splendor
ISBN 978-1-907661-98-3

Paul Pearsall, Ph.D. —
Super Joy
ISBN 978-1-908733-16-0

**All titles available as eBooks, and selected titles available in Hardback and
Audiobook formats from www.whitecrowbooks.com**

Lightning Source UK Ltd.
Milton Keynes UK
UKHW041457091219
355041UK00008B/2397/P